Home-Tested
RECIPE COLLECTION

Publications International, Ltd.

Favorite Brand Name Recipes at www.fbnr.com

Pictured on the front cover *(clockwise from top):* Beef in Wine Sauce *(page 8)*, Raspberry Cream Pie *(page 214)*, Easy Vegetable Beef Stew *(page 12)* and Cha-Cha-Cha Casserole *(page 152)*.

Pictured on the back cover *(top to bottom):* Caramel Apple Bread Pudding with Cinnamon Cream *(page 318)*, Mediterranean Vegetable Bake *(page 192)* and Southwest Spaghetti Squash *(page 150)*.

ISBN: 0-7853-9672-1

Library of Congress Control Number: 2003109990

Manufactured in China.

8 7 6 5 4 3 2 1

Microwave Cooking: Microwave ovens vary in wattage. Use the cooking times as guidelines and check for doneness before adding more time.

CONTENTS

THE BASICS

Finally, a cookbook filled with recipes from cooks just like you! You'll find recipes with familiar, easy-to-find ingredients, and main dishes and desserts your family is sure to love. In other words, recipes you'll want to make again and again. These home-tested recipes were gathered from home cooks from across America in a series of contests previously sponsored by this publisher. Now they've been compiled into one great cookbook. You can choose from the best family-pleasing casseroles and convenient slow cooker meals—plus fabulous pies, tasty cakes and easy desserts.

Slow Cooker Basics

Considering the hectic pace of today's lifestyles, it's no wonder so many people have rediscovered the time-saving kitchen helper, the slow cooker. Spend a few minutes preparing the ingredients, turn on the slow cooker and relax. Low heat and long cooking times take the stress out of meal preparation. Leave for work or a day of leisure and come home to a hot, delicious meal.

There are two types of slow cookers. The most common models have heat coils circling the crockery inset, allowing heat to surround the food and cook evenly. Two settings, LOW (about 200°F) and HIGH (about 300°F) regulate cooking temperatures. One hour on HIGH equals 2 to 2½ hours on LOW. Less common models have heat coils on the bottom and have adjustable thermostats. If you own this type, consult your manufacturer's instructions for advice on converting the recipes in this publication.

Tips and Techniques

Filling the Slow Cooker: Manufacturers recommend that slow cookers should be one-half to three-quarters full for best results.

Keep a Lid On It: A slow cooker can take as long as twenty minutes to regain heat lost when the cover is removed. If the recipe calls for stirring or checking the dish near the end of the cooking time, replace the cover as quickly as you can. Otherwise, resist the urge to remove the cover.

Adapting Recipes: If you'd like to adapt your own favorite recipe to a slow cooker, you'll need to follow a few guidelines. First, try to find a similar slow cooker recipe in this publication or the manufacturer's guide. Note the cooking times, amount of liquid, quantity and size of meat and vegetable pieces. Because the slow cooker captures moisture, you will want to reduce the amount of liquid, often by as much as half. Add dairy products, such as milk, sour cream and cheese, near the end of the cooking time so they do not curdle. Evaporated milk and cream are good substitutes for milk, because they can withstand long cooking in a slow cooker. Follow this chart to estimate the cooking time you will need:

Conventional Recipe	Cook on Low	Cook on High
30 to 45 minutes	6 to 10 hours	3 to 4 hours
50 minutes to 3 hours	8 to 15 hours	4 to 6 hours

Selecting the Right Meat: You can, and in fact should, use tougher, inexpensive cuts of meat. Top-quality cuts, such as loin chops or filet mignon, fall apart during long cooking periods and therefore are not good choices to use in the slow cooker. You will be amazed to find even the toughest cuts come out fork-tender and flavorful.

Reducing the Fat: The slow cooker can help you make lower-fat meals because you won't be cooking in fat as you do when you sauté and stir-fry. Many recipes call for trimming excess fat from meat. If you do use fatty cuts of meat, such as ribs, brown them first on top of the range to cook off excess fat before adding them to the slow cooker. Chicken skin tends to shrivel and curl in the slow cooker, so most recipes call for skinless chicken. If you use skin-on pieces, brown them before adding them to the slow cooker.

Cutting Your Vegetables: Vegetables often take longer to cook than meats. Cut vegetables into small, thin pieces and place them near the bottom of the slow cooker. Follow the recipe instructions and cut vegetables to the proper size so they will cook in the amount of time given.

Food Safety Tips: If you do any advance preparation, such as trimming meat or cutting vegetables, make sure to cover and refrigerate the food until you are ready to start cooking. Store uncooked meats and vegetables separately. If you are preparing meat, poultry or fish, remember to wash your cutting board, utensils and hands with hot, soapy water before touching other food. Never cook frozen raw chicken or turkey pieces in a slow cooker. Instead, thaw in the refrigerator before cooking them in a slow cooker.

Once the food is cooked, don't keep it in the slow cooker too long. Foods need to be kept cooler than 40°F or hotter than 140°F to avoid growth of harmful bacteria. Remove food to a clean container, cover and refrigerate as soon as possible. For large amounts of leftovers, it is best to divide them into several containers so they will cool faster. Do not reheat leftovers in the slow cooker. Use a microwave oven, the range top or the oven for reheating.

Casserole Basics

Casseroles are America's true comfort food. Everyone loves creamy macaroni and cheese, hearty manicotti, and spicy chicken and rice. A whole meal in one dish means less time preparing and cleaning up. You can always count on a casserole to win rave reviews at the dinner table.

Casserole cookware comes in a variety of shapes, sizes and materials that fall into two general descriptions. They can be either deep, round containers with handles and tight-fitting lids or square and rectangular baking dishes. Casseroles are made of glass, ceramic or metal. When making a casserole, it's important to bake the casserole in the proper size dish so that the ingredients cook evenly in the time specified.

Size Unknown?

If the size of the casserole or baking dish isn't marked on the bottom of the dish, it can be measured to determine the size.

• Round and oval casseroles are measured by volume, not inches, and are listed by quart capacity. Fill a measuring cup with water and pour it into the empty casserole. Repeat until the casserole is filled with water, keeping track of the amount of water added. The amount of water is equivalent to the size of the dish.

• Square and rectangular baking dishes are usually measured in inches. If the dimensions are not marked in the bottom of a baking dish, use a ruler to measure on top from the inside of one edge to the inside of the opposite edge. Repeat to determine the other dimension.

Dessert Basics

Delight your family and friends with homemade desserts from this collection of recipes. You'll find over 130 great-tasting pies, cakes and desserts in this book. Like the home cooks whose recipes fill this cookbook, you'll want to pass these wonderful home-tested recipes on to your friends. If you're a beginning baker, follow these basic guidelines to help insure success.

• Read the entire recipe before you begin to be sure you have all the necessary ingredients.

• Preheat the oven. Check the oven temperature for accuracy with an oven thermometer.

• Remove butter, margarine and cream cheese from the refrigerator to soften, if necessary. Toast and chop nuts, peel and slice fruit, and melt chocolate before beginning to mix ingredients.

• Measure ingredients accurately and assemble them in the order they are listed in the recipe. Use glass or plastic measures with spouts to measure liquids. Check the measurements at eye level. To measure dry ingredients, fill standard spoon and cup measures to overflowing, then level off with a spatula or the flat edge of a knife.

Toasting Nuts

Toasting nuts brings out their flavor. Spread the nuts in a single layer on a baking sheet. Bake in a preheated 325°F oven for 8 to 10 minutes or until golden, stirring occasionally for even toasting. The nuts will darken and become crisper as they cool. To toast a small amount of nuts, place them in a dry skillet over low heat. Stir constantly for 2 to 4 minutes or until the nuts darken slightly.

Toasting Coconut

Spread flaked coconut out in a thin layer on a baking sheet. Bake in a preheated 325°F oven for 7 to 10 minutes. Stir the coconut occasionally for even browning and to prevent burning.

FABULOUS MEATS

beef in wine sauce

Tamara Frazier, Escondido, CA

4 pounds boneless beef chuck roast, cut into 1½- to 2-inch cubes
2 tablespoons garlic powder
2 cans (10¾ ounces each) condensed golden mushroom soup, undiluted
1 can (8 ounces) sliced mushrooms, drained
¾ cup dry sherry
1 envelope (about 1 ounce) dry onion soup mix
1 bag (20 ounces) frozen sliced carrots

1. Preheat oven to 325°F. Spray heavy 4-quart casserole or Dutch oven with nonstick cooking spray.

2. Sprinkle beef with garlic powder. Place in prepared casserole.

3. Combine soup, mushrooms, sherry and onion soup mix in medium bowl. Pour over meat; mix well.

4. Cover and bake 3 hours or until meat is very tender. Add carrots during last 15 minutes of baking.

Makes 6 to 8 servings

beef in wine sauce

it's a keeper casserole

Carol A. Stone, Waverly, TN

  1 tablespoon vegetable oil
½ cup chopped onion
¼ cup chopped green bell pepper
  1 clove garlic, minced
  2 tablespoons all-purpose flour
  1 teaspoon sugar
½ teaspoon salt
½ teaspoon dried basil leaves
½ teaspoon black pepper
  1 can (about 16 ounces) whole tomatoes, cut up
  1 package (about 16 ounces) frozen fully-cooked meatballs
1½ cups cooked vegetables (any combination)
  1 teaspoon beef bouillon granules
  1 teaspoon Worcestershire sauce
  1 can refrigerated buttermilk biscuits

1. Preheat oven to 400°F. Heat oil in large saucepan. Cook and stir onion, bell pepper and garlic over medium heat until vegetables are tender.

2. Stir in flour, sugar, salt, basil and black pepper. Slowly blend in tomatoes, meatballs, vegetables, bouillon and Worcestershire sauce. Cook and stir until slightly thickened and bubbling; pour into 2-quart casserole.

3. Unroll biscuits; place on top of casserole. Bake, uncovered, 15 minutes or until biscuits are golden.

Makes 4 servings

it's a keeper casserole

easy vegetable beef stew

Jane Lindeman, Skokie, IL

   1 pound beef for stew, cut into 1-inch pieces
   1 can (14½ ounces) diced tomatoes, undrained
   1 medium onion, cut into 8 wedges
   4 carrots, cut into 1-inch pieces
   1 green or red bell pepper, diced
   1 rib celery, sliced
   1 teaspoon Italian seasoning
   ½ teaspoon salt
   ½ teaspoon black pepper
   1 tablespoon vegetable oil
   1 package (8 ounces) sliced mushrooms

1. Combine beef pieces, tomatoes with juice and onion in Dutch oven. Cover tightly; bake at 325°F 1 hour.

2. Add carrots, bell pepper, celery, Italian seasoning, salt and black pepper to beef mixture; stir. Cover; bake an additional 45 minutes or until beef and carrots are tender.

3. Heat oil in large skillet over medium heat. Add mushrooms; cook and stir 10 minutes or until lightly browned and tender. Stir mushrooms into beef stew. Adjust seasonings to taste.

Makes 4 servings

Variation: Two unpeeled medium red potatoes, cut into 2-inch pieces, may be added with carrots.

easy vegetable beef stew

athens casserole

Barbara J. Dickinson, Harbor City, NJ

  2 tablespoons vegetable oil
1½ pounds eggplant, peeled, cut crosswise into ¼-inch slices
1½ pounds ground beef
  2 cups chopped onions
  1 medium green bell pepper, cut into strips
  1 medium yellow bell pepper, cut into strips
  1 medium red bell pepper, cut into strips
  ¼ cup chopped fresh parsley
  ¼ cup red wine
  1 teaspoon garlic powder
  1 teaspoon ground cinnamon
    Salt and black pepper
  2 cans (28 ounces each) stewed tomatoes
  8 ounces feta cheese, crumbled
  4 eggs, beaten
  ½ cup bread crumbs

1. Preheat oven to 350°F.

2. Heat oil in large skillet over medium-high heat. Add eggplant and brown on both sides, 5 to 7 minutes; set aside on paper towels to drain.

3. In same skillet, cook and stir ground beef, onions and bell peppers over medium heat until onions are transparent and beef is browned. Add parsley, wine, garlic powder and cinnamon; mix well. Season with salt and black pepper.

4. Pour ⅓ of tomatoes into 13×9-inch baking dish. Layer with ⅓ eggplant, ⅓ beef mixture and ⅓ cheese. Repeat layers twice. Pour eggs over top and sprinkle with bread crumbs.

5. Bake 45 minutes or until heated through and bubbly.   *Makes 10 servings*

lemon pork chops

Ginger Williams, Lauderdale, MS

1 tablespoon vegetable oil
4 boneless pork chops
3 cans (8 ounces each) tomato sauce
1 large onion, quartered and sliced (optional)
1 large green bell pepper, cut into strips
1 tablespoon lemon-pepper seasoning
1 tablespoon Worcestershire sauce
1 large lemon, quartered

Slow Cooker Directions

1. Heat oil in large skillet over medium-low heat. Brown pork chops on both sides. Drain excess fat. Place pork into slow cooker.

2. Combine tomato sauce, onion, if desired, bell pepper, lemon-pepper seasoning and Worcestershire sauce in slow cooker. Squeeze juice from lemon quarters over mixture; drop squeezed peels into slow cooker. Cover; cook on LOW 6 to 8 hours or until pork is tender.

Makes 4 servings

Ginger says: Serve with rolls, green beans and mashed potatoes. Use the spiced-up tomato sauce for gravy on the potatoes. (If you like, add an extra can of tomato sauce to the slow cooker for even more gravy.) Excellent meal!

spicy beefy noodles

Marlene Roberts, Moore, OK

1½ pounds ground beef
1 small onion, minced
1 small clove garlic, minced
1 tablespoon chili powder
1 teaspoon paprika
⅛ teaspoon *each* of dried basil leaves, dill weed, dried thyme leaves and dried marjoram leaves
    Salt and black pepper
1 can (10 ounces) diced tomatoes with green chilies, undrained
1 can (8 ounces) tomato sauce
1 cup water
3 tablespoons Worcestershire sauce
1 package (about 10 ounces) egg noodles, cooked according to package directions
½ cup (2 ounces) *each* shredded Cheddar, mozzarella, pepper Jack and provolone cheeses

1. Cook and stir ground beef, onion and garlic in large skillet over medium heat until meat is no longer pink, stirring to separate meat; drain well. Add chili powder, paprika, basil, dill, thyme and marjoram. Season with salt and pepper. Cook and stir 2 minutes.

2. Add tomatoes with juice, tomato sauce, water and Worcestershire sauce; mix well. Simmer, covered, 20 minutes.

3. In microwavable 2-quart casserole combine meat mixture and noodles. Mix shredded cheeses and sprinkle evenly over top.

4. Microwave at HIGH 3 minutes. Let stand 5 minutes. Microwave 3 minutes longer or until cheeses melt.

Makes 6 servings

spicy beefy noodles

old-fashioned cabbage rolls

Arnita Jones, McKenzie, TN

½ pound ground beef
½ pound ground veal
½ pound ground pork
1 small onion, chopped
2 eggs, lightly beaten
½ cup dry bread crumbs
1 teaspoon salt
1 teaspoon molasses
¼ teaspoon ground ginger
¼ teaspoon ground nutmeg
¼ teaspoon ground allspice
1 large head cabbage, separated into leaves
3 cups boiling water
¼ cup butter or margarine
½ cup milk, or more as needed
1 tablespoon cornstarch

1. Combine meats and onion in large bowl. Combine eggs, bread crumbs, salt, molasses, ginger, nutmeg and allspice in medium bowl; mix well. Add to meat mixture and mix well.

2. Drop cabbage leaves into boiling water for 3 minutes. Remove with slotted spoon, reserving ½ cup of boiling liquid.

3. Preheat oven to 375°F. Place about 2 tablespoons of meat mixture about 1 inch from stem end of each leaf. Fold sides in and roll up, fastening with toothpicks, if necessary.

4. Heat butter in large skillet over medium-high heat. Add cabbage rolls (3 or 4 at a time) to skillet and brown on all sides. Arrange rolls, seam side down, in single layer in casserole. Combine reserved boiling liquid with butter remaining in skillet; pour over cabbage rolls.

continued on page 20

old-fashioned cabbage rolls

old-fashioned cabbage rolls, continued

5. Bake 1 hour. Remove and carefully drain accumulated pan juices into measuring cup. Return cabbage rolls to oven. Add enough milk to pan juices to equal 1 cup.

6. Pour milk mixture into small saucepan; stir in cornstarch and bring to a boil, stirring constantly until sauce is thickened. Pour over cabbage rolls. Bake 15 minutes more or until sauce is browned and cabbage is very tender.

Makes 8 servings

beef boogie woogie

Ruth Ann Haskins, Hoquiam, WA

1 can (10¾ ounces) condensed cream of mushroom soup, undiluted
½ cup chicken broth
1 package (1 ounce) dry onion soup mix
½ teaspoon dried thyme leaves
2 pounds lean beef stew meat
2 cups baby carrots
8 ounces mushrooms, sliced

Slow Cooker Directions

1. Combine mushroom soup, broth, soup mix and thyme in slow cooker; mix well.

2. Add remaining ingredients and stir until evenly coated. Cover; cook on HIGH 4 hours or on LOW 8 to 10 hours or until meat is tender.

Makes 8 servings

Ruth Ann says: Serve this dish over noodles or with mashed potatoes. Sprinkle with parsley before serving.

spanish rice & squash
Charlotte Sue Taylor, Midway, WV

**2 small yellow summer squash, cut into ¼-inch slices
1 small zucchini, cut into ¼-inch slices
1 package (about 12 ounces) Spanish rice mix
2 cups water
1 can (about 14 ounces) diced tomatoes, undrained
1 can (about 4 ounces) sliced mushrooms, drained
3 tablespoons butter, melted
1 pound smoked sausage, cut into 4-inch pieces
1 can (about 3 ounces) French fried onions
1 cup (4 ounces) shredded mozzarella cheese**

1. Preheat oven to 350°F. Coat 3-quart casserole with nonstick cooking spray. Place sliced squash and zucchini in prepared casserole.

2. Combine rice mix, water, tomatoes with juice, mushrooms and butter in medium bowl; stir well. Pour over squash; top with sausage.

3. Cover; bake 20 minutes. Remove from oven; uncover and place onions around edge of casserole. Sprinkle cheese in center. Bake, uncovered, 5 to 10 minutes more or until cheese melts.

Makes 4 to 6 servings

mushroom-beef stew

Dana R. Moore, Rochester, NY

1 pound beef stew meat
1 can (10¾ ounces) condensed cream of mushroom soup, undiluted
2 cans (4 ounces each) sliced mushrooms, drained
1 package (1 ounce) dry onion soup mix
  Hot cooked noodles

Slow Cooker Directions

Combine all ingredients except noodles in slow cooker. Cover; cook on LOW 8 to 10 hours. Serve over noodles. Garnish as desired.

Makes 4 servings

Dana says: Serve this stew over hot cooked seasoned noodles or rice.

simple slow cooker pork roast

Andrea Shuster, Plantsville, CT

4 to 5 red potatoes, cut into bite-size pieces
4 carrots, cut into bite-size pieces
1 marinated pork loin roast (3 to 4 pounds)
½ cup water
1 package (10 ounces) frozen baby peas

Slow Cooker Directions

Place potatoes, carrots and pork roast in slow cooker. (If necessary, cut roast in half to fit in slow cooker.) Add water. Cover; cook on LOW 6 to 8 hours or until vegetables are tender. Add peas during last hour of cooking. Season to taste.

Makes 6 servings

mushroom-beef stew

honey ribs

Donna Urbanek, Levittown, PA

   1 can (10¾ ounces) condensed beef consommé
   ½ cup water
   3 tablespoons soy sauce
   2 tablespoons honey
   2 tablespoons maple syrup
   2 tablespoons barbecue sauce
   ½ teaspoon dry mustard
   2 pounds pork baby back ribs, trimmed

Slow Cooker Directions

1. Combine all ingredients except ribs in slow cooker; mix well.

2. Cut ribs into 3- to 4-rib portions. Add ribs to slow cooker. (If ribs are especially fatty, broil 10 minutes before adding to slow cooker.) Cover; cook on LOW 6 to 8 hours or on HIGH 4 to 6 hours or until ribs are tender. Cut into individual ribs. Serve with sauce. *Makes 4 servings*

Donna says: These ribs are delicious alone, but are even better served with rice.

honey ribs

indian-style lamb and chick-peas

Marilyn Pocius, Oak Park, IL

2 tablespoons butter, divided
1 onion, chopped
3 cloves garlic, chopped
2 teaspoons finely chopped fresh ginger
1 pound ground lamb
2 tablespoons lemon juice
   Salt and black pepper
1 pound (about 3 medium) fresh tomatoes, diced
1 tablespoon curry powder
½ teaspoon ground red pepper
⅛ teaspoon ground cinnamon
⅛ teaspoon ground nutmeg
2 cans (about 15 ounces each) chick-peas, rinsed and drained
¾ cup plain yogurt (not nonfat)
½ cup dry bread crumbs

1. Preheat oven to 350°F. Melt 1 tablespoon butter in large skillet. Cook and stir onion, garlic and ginger over medium-high heat for 2 minutes until onion begins to soften. Add lamb; cook, stirring to break up meat, until no longer pink. Season with salt and black pepper.

2. Add tomatoes, curry powder, red pepper, cinnamon and nutmeg; cook and stir 5 minutes until well combined. Remove from heat. Add chick-peas and yogurt; stir to combine.

3. Transfer mixture to 2- to 2½-quart casserole. Sprinkle bread crumbs on top and dot with remaining 1 tablespoon butter. Bake 30 minutes or until bubbly and lightly browned.

Makes 6 to 8 servings

chili verde

Pam Egendorfer, Newbury Park, CA

1 tablespoon vegetable oil
1 to 2 pounds boneless pork chops
   Sliced carrots (enough to cover bottom of slow cooker)
1 jar (24 ounces) mild green chili salsa
   Chopped onion (optional)

Slow Cooker Directions

1. Heat oil in large skillet over medium-low heat. Brown pork on both sides. Drain excess fat.

2. Place carrot slices in bottom of slow cooker. Place pork on top of carrots. Pour salsa over chops. Add onion to taste, if desired. Cover; cook on HIGH 6 to 8 hours.　　　*Makes 4 to 8 servings*

Pam says: If desired, shred the pork and serve it with tortillas.

Helpful Hint: **Browning meats and poultry before cooking in the slow cooker is not necessary, but it can enhance the flavor and appearance of the finished dish.**

easy moroccan casserole

April Parmelee, Anaheim, CA

2 tablespoons vegetable oil
1 pound pork stew meat, cut into 1-inch cubes
½ cup chopped onion
3 tablespoons all-purpose flour
1 can (about 14 ounces) diced tomatoes, undrained
¼ cup water
1 teaspoon *each* ground ginger, ground cumin and ground cinnamon
½ teaspoon sugar
½ teaspoon salt
½ teaspoon black pepper
2 medium unpeeled red potatoes, cut into ½-inch pieces
1 large sweet potato, peeled and cut into ½-inch pieces
1 cup frozen lima beans, thawed and drained
1 cup frozen cut green beans, thawed and drained
¾ cup sliced carrots
   Pita bread

1. Preheat oven to 325°F.

2. Heat oil in large skillet over medium-high heat. Add pork and onion; cook, stirring occasionally, until pork is browned on all sides. Sprinkle flour over meat mixture, stir until flour has absorbed pan juices. Cook 2 minutes more.

3. Stir in tomatoes with juice, water, ginger, cumin, cinnamon, sugar, salt and pepper. Transfer mixture to 2-quart casserole. Bake 30 minutes.

4. Stir in potatoes, sweet potato, lima beans, green beans and carrots. Cover; bake 1 hour or until potatoes are tender. Serve with pita bread. *Makes 6 servings*

easy moroccan casserole

slow cooker meatloaf

Carolyn Stanley, Middletown, DE

1½ **pounds ground beef**
¾ **cup milk**
⅔ **cup fine dry bread crumbs**
2 **eggs, beaten**
2 **tablespoons minced onion**
1 **teaspoon salt**
½ **teaspoon ground sage**
½ **cup ketchup**
2 **tablespoons brown sugar**
1 **teaspoon dry mustard**

Slow Cooker Directions

1. Combine beef, milk, bread crumbs, eggs, onion, salt and sage in large bowl. Shape into ball and place in slow cooker. Cover; cook on LOW 5 to 6 hours.

2. Fifteen minutes before serving, combine ketchup, brown sugar and mustard in small bowl. Pour over meatloaf. Cover; cook on HIGH 15 minutes.
Makes 6 servings

Carolyn says: This is so good, I serve it to company!

slow cooker meatloaf

slow-cooked smothered steak

Lynda McCormick, Burkburnett, TX

⅓ cup all-purpose flour
1 teaspoon garlic salt
½ teaspoon black pepper
1½ pounds beef chuck or round steak, cut into strips
1 large onion, sliced
1 to 2 medium green bell peppers, cut into strips
1 can (4 ounces) sliced mushrooms, drained
¼ cup teriyaki sauce
1 package (10 ounces) frozen French-style green beans

Slow Cooker Directions

1. Combine flour, garlic salt and black pepper in medium bowl. Add steak strips, tossing to coat with flour mixture. Place steak into slow cooker.

2. Layer remaining ingredients in slow cooker. Cover; cook on HIGH 1 hour. Reduce heat to LOW; cook on LOW 8 hours (or leave on HIGH 5 hours). *Makes 6 servings*

Lynda says: Serve over hot steamed white rice. This is a great recipe to double (use a 12-ounce can of mushrooms when doing so). It will fill a 6-quart slow cooker if doubling or a 3½-quart model if making a single recipe. The lid may touch the green beans, but don't worry about it overflowing, because the contents will settle.

beefy texas cheddar bake

Peter Halferty, Corpus Christi, TX

1½ **pounds 90% lean ground beef**
1 **cup chopped onion**
2 **cans (10¾ ounces each) condensed tomato soup, preferably Mexican-style, undiluted**
2 **cups beef broth**
1 **box (6 ounces) corn bread stuffing mix**
4 **tablespoons margarine or butter, melted**
2 **teaspoons ground cumin**
2 **teaspoons ground chili powder**
2 **cups (8 ounces) shredded Mexican-style cheese**

1. Preheat oven to 350°F. Grease 3-quart casserole.

2. Cook and stir beef and onion in large skillet over medium heat 5 minutes or until meat is no longer pink; drain fat. Spoon meat into prepared casserole.

3. Mix soup, broth, stuffing mix, margarine, cumin and chili powder in large bowl until combined. Spoon evenly over beef mixture. Top with cheese.

4. Bake 30 minutes or until heated through.

Makes 8 servings

potato sausage casserole

Billie Olofson, Des Moines, IA

> 1 pound bulk pork sausage or ground pork
> 1 can (10¾ ounces) condensed cream of mushroom soup, undiluted
> ¾ cup milk
> ½ cup chopped onion
> ½ teaspoon salt
> ¼ teaspoon black pepper
> 3 cups sliced potatoes
> ½ tablespoon butter
> 1½ cups (6 ounces) shredded Cheddar cheese

1. Preheat oven to 350°F. Spray 1½-quart casserole with nonstick cooking spray; set aside.

2. Cook sausage in large skillet over medium-high heat, stirring to separate, until no longer pink; drain fat.

3. Stir together soup, milk, onion, salt and pepper in medium bowl.

4. Place half of potatoes in prepared casserole; top with half of soup mixture, then with half of sausage. Repeat layers, ending with sausage. Dot with butter.

5. Cover pan with foil. Bake 1¼ to 1½ hours until potatoes are tender. Uncover; sprinkle with cheese. Return to oven; bake until cheese is melted and bubbly. *Makes 6 servings*

potato sausage casserole

swiss steak

Amy Rivera, Arlington, VA

   1 onion, cut into thick rings
   1 clove garlic, minced
   1 beef round steak (about 2 pounds), cut into 8 pieces
     All-purpose flour
     Salt
     Black pepper
   1 can (28 ounces) whole tomatoes, undrained
   1 can (10¾ ounces) condensed tomato soup, undrained
   3 medium unpeeled potatoes, diced
   1 package (16 ounces) frozen peas and carrots
   1 cup sliced celery
     Additional vegetables

Slow Cooker Directions

1. Place onion and garlic in slow cooker.

2. Dredge steak in flour seasoned with salt and pepper. Shake off excess flour. Place steak in slow cooker. Add tomatoes with juice. Cover with tomato soup. Add potatoes, peas and carrots, celery and any additional vegetables. Cover; cook on HIGH 4 to 6 hours or until meat and potatoes are tender.   *Makes 8 servings*

Amy says: I sometimes add corn or green beans. This recipe is very easy and definitely a family favorite!

swiss steak

tender chuck roast with vegetables

Cyndi White, Shreveport, LA

1 boneless beef chuck shoulder roast (2½ to 3 pounds)
  Salt
  Black pepper
  Garlic powder
6 large carrots
3 ribs celery
3 medium potatoes, peeled
1 large onion
2 cans (14 ounces each) beef broth with onions
1 cup wine
⅓ cup water
2 tablespoons cornstarch

Slow Cooker Directions

1. Place roast in slow cooker; season with salt, pepper and garlic powder to taste.

2. Cut carrots and celery into thirds. Quarter potatoes. Cut onion into wedges. Add all vegetables to slow cooker; sprinkle with salt and pepper to taste.

3. Pour broth and wine over vegetables and beef. Cover top tightly with foil. Cover foil with lid; cook on LOW 8 to 10 hours.

4. Remove meat and vegetables to serving dish; keep warm. Combine water and cornstarch in small bowl: stir into liquid. Cook on HIGH 15 minutes or until juices are thickened. Serve gravy with meat and vegetables.

Makes 6 servings

curried pork pot

Gina Brittain, Schenectady, NY

　　1 can (10¾ ounces) condensed cream of chicken soup
　　1 cup evaporated skimmed milk or water
　　1 medium onion, chopped
　½ cup raisins
　　1 tablespoon mild curry powder
　　1 tablespoon dried parsley flakes
　　1 teaspoon minced garlic
　　1 pound boneless country-style pork ribs
　　　Salt
　　　Black pepper
　　　Hot cooked rice, pasta or egg noodles

Slow Cooker Directions

Combine soup, milk, onion, raisins, curry, parsley and garlic in large bowl; mix well. Add pork, stirring to coat. Place mixture in slow cooker. Cover; cook on LOW 6 to 8 hours or on HIGH 3 to 4 hours. Stir in salt and pepper to taste. Serve over rice, pasta or noodles. *Makes 6 servings*

beef roll-ups

Mary Schrank, Racine, WI

1 boneless beef round steak, ½ inch thick (1½ pounds)
4 slices bacon
½ cup diced green bell pepper
¼ cup diced onion
¼ cup diced celery
1 can (10 ounces) beef gravy

Slow Cooker Directions

1. Cut steak into 4 pieces. Place 1 bacon slice on each piece.

2. Combine bell pepper, onion and celery in medium bowl. Place about ¼ cup mixture on each piece of meat. Roll up meat; secure with wooden toothpicks.

3. Place beef rolls in slow cooker. Pour gravy evenly over top. Cover; cook on LOW 8 to 10 hours. Skim fat; discard.

Makes 4 servings

Mary says: Serve with mashed potatoes or over rice.

beef roll-up

simply delicious pork
Carol Morris, Auburn, IN

  1½ pounds boneless pork loin, cut into 6 pieces *or* 6 boneless pork loin chops
    4 medium Yellow Delicious apples, sliced
    3 tablespoons brown sugar
    1 teaspoon cinnamon
    ½ teaspoon salt

Slow Cooker Directions

1. Place pork in slow cooker. Cover with apples.

2. Combine brown sugar, cinnamon and salt in small bowl; sprinkle over apples. Cover; cook on LOW 6 to 8 hours. *Makes 6 servings*

easy beef stew
Julie Miller-Longo, St. Charles, IL

  1½ to 2 pounds beef stew meat
    4 medium potatoes, cubed
    4 carrots, cut into 1½-inch pieces, *or* 4 cups baby carrots
    1 medium onion, cut into 8 pieces
    2 cans (8 ounces each) tomato sauce
    1 teaspoon salt
    ½ teaspoon black pepper

Slow Cooker Directions

Combine all ingredients in slow cooker. Cover; cook on LOW 8 to 10 hours or until vegetables are tender. *Makes 6 to 8 servings*

simply delicious pork

saucy braised beef

Marti Munns, Redwood City, CA

Hot cooked noodles
2 pounds boneless beef top round steak, cut into bite-size pieces
1 tablespoon mixed dried herbs
Salt
Black pepper
2 tablespoons vegetable oil
2 cups baby carrots
1 large yellow onion, thinly sliced
1 medium zucchini, cut into 1-inch slices
2 tablespoons minced garlic
1 teaspoon dried oregano leaves
1 can (8 ounces) tomato sauce
1 can (6 ounces) tomato paste
½ cup dark molasses
2 tablespoons red wine vinegar
2 teaspoons hot pepper sauce

Slow Cooker Directions

1. Lightly season beef with mixed herbs, salt and pepper to taste. Heat oil in Dutch oven or large skillet over medium-low heat. Brown meat on all sides. Drain fat; discard. Place beef in slow cooker.

2. Add carrots, onion, zucchini, garlic and oregano to Dutch oven. Cook over medium-low heat 4 to 5 minutes or until onion is tender, stirring occasionally. Add vegetable mixture and remaining ingredients to slow cooker; mix well. Cover; cook on LOW 8 to 10 hours. Serve over noodles.

Makes 4 to 6 servings

sauerkraut pork ribs

Chris Brill, Shorewood, WI

 1 tablespoon vegetable oil
 3 to 4 pounds pork country-style ribs
 1 large onion, thinly sliced
 1 teaspoon caraway seeds
 ½ teaspoon garlic powder
 ¼ to ½ teaspoon black pepper
 ¾ cup water
 1 jar (about 28 ounces) sauerkraut
 6 medium potatoes, quartered

Slow Cooker Directions

1. Heat oil in large skillet over medium-low heat. Brown ribs on all sides; transfer ribs to slow cooker. Drain excess fat.

2. Add onion to skillet; cook until tender. Add caraway seeds, garlic powder and pepper; cook 15 minutes. Transfer onion mixture to slow cooker.

3. Add water to skillet and scrape bottom of pan. Pour pan juices into slow cooker. Partially drain sauerkraut, leaving some liquid; pour over meat in slow cooker. Top with potatoes. Cover; cook on LOW 6 to 8 hours or until potatoes are tender, stirring once during cooking.   *Makes 12 servings*

emily's goulash

Emily Hale, Chicago, IL

½ cup all-purpose flour
3 teaspoons salt, divided
2 teaspoons pepper, divided
2 pounds boneless beef chuck shoulder, cut into bite-size pieces
¼ cup plus 2 tablespoons vegetable oil, divided
2 shallots, finely chopped
3 cloves garlic, finely chopped
1 large can (about 28 ounces) diced tomatoes, undrained
1 tablespoon paprika
3½ cups water
1 teaspoon *each* dried parsley leaves and dried thyme leaves
2 bay leaves
3 tablespoons sour cream

1. Combine flour, 2 teaspoons salt and 1 teaspoon pepper in shallow bowl. Heat large ovenproof Dutch oven over medium-high heat. Add ¼ cup vegetable oil. Dip pieces of beef into flour mixture; shake off excess flour. Brown beef in batches in Dutch oven. Do not crowd pan. Remove beef; set aside. Drain fat and wipe out pan.

2. Preheat oven to 325°F. Add remaining 2 tablespoons oil to Dutch oven; cook and stir shallots and garlic over medium heat about 2 minutes. Add tomatoes and paprika; simmer 2 minutes. Add beef, accumulated juices, water and herbs. Cover; bake about 1½ hours until beef is tender.

3. Remove from oven; simmer over medium heat 20 minutes, stirring occasionally. Reduce heat to low and stir in sour cream. Cook and stir until liquid has reduced to sauce-like consistency, about 20 minutes. Stir in remaining 1 teaspoon salt and 1 teaspoon pepper. Remove and discard bay leaves.

Makes 4 to 6 servings

Emily says: Serve this over buttered egg noodles sprinkled with parsley.

emily's goulash

delicious ham & cheese puff pie

Roxanne Chan, Albany, CA

2 cups (about 1 pound) diced cooked ham
1 package (10 ounces) frozen chopped spinach, thawed and squeezed dry
½ cup diced red bell pepper
4 green onions, sliced
3 eggs
¾ cup all-purpose flour
¾ cup (3 ounces) shredded Swiss cheese
¾ cup milk
1 tablespoon prepared mustard
1 teaspoon grated lemon peel
1 teaspoon dried dill weed
½ teaspoon garlic salt
½ teaspoon ground black pepper
Dill sprigs and lemon slices (optional)

1. Preheat oven to 425°F. Grease 2-quart casserole.

2. Combine ham, spinach, bell pepper and onions in prepared casserole.

3. Beat eggs in medium bowl. Stir in remaining ingredients except dill and lemon slices; pour over ham mixture.

4. Bake 30 to 35 minutes or until puffed and browned. Cut into wedges and garnish with dill sprigs and lemon slices, if desired.

Makes 4 to 6 servings

delicious ham & cheese puff pie

jackpot casserole

Ann C. Port, Southborough, MA

2 tablespoons butter or olive oil
2 medium onions, chopped
2 ribs celery, chopped
1 package (8 ounces) mushrooms, sliced *or* 1 can (4 ounces) sliced mushrooms, drained
1 to 1½ pounds ground beef
1 can (4 ounces) sliced olives, drained
1½ cups cooked rice
1 can (8 ounces) tomato sauce
Salt and pepper

1. Preheat oven to 350°F.

2. Melt butter in large skillet over medium heat. Add onions and celery; cook and stir until almost tender. Add mushrooms; cook and stir until vegetables are soft.

3. In separate medium skillet, cook beef over medium-high heat 10 minutes or until no longer pink, stirring to separate meat. Pour off fat.

4. Combine vegetable mixture, beef, olives and rice in 3- to 4-quart casserole. Add tomato sauce, salt and pepper. Mix well.

5. Cover and bake 1 hour or until heated through.   *Makes 4 to 6 servings*

hawaiian pork chops

Brenda Imler, Reddick, FL

1 can (20 ounces) crushed pineapple, undrained
2 large sweet potatoes, peeled and thinly sliced
1 teaspoon cinnamon
6 to 8 boneless pork chops
½ teaspoon salt
½ teaspoon black pepper

1. Preheat oven to 350°F. Grease 13×9-inch casserole.

2. Place crushed pineapple in prepared casserole. Layer sweet potatoes over pineapple and sprinkle with cinnamon. Place pork chops on top and season with salt and pepper.

3. Cover with foil and bake about 50 to 60 minutes or until sweet potatoes are tender. Remove from oven. *Increase oven temperature to 400°F.* Remove foil and return casserole to oven. Bake about 10 minutes until liquid is reduced and chops are browned. *Makes 6 to 8 servings*

peppered beef tips

Barbara Messman, Birmingham, AL

1 pound beef sirloin or round tip steaks
2 cloves garlic, minced
  Black pepper
1 can (10¾ ounces) condensed French onion soup
1 can (10¾ ounces) condensed cream of mushroom soup, undiluted
  Hot cooked noodles or rice

Slow Cooker Directions

Place beef tips in slow cooker. Sprinkle with garlic and pepper. Pour soups over beef. Cover; cook on LOW 8 to 10 hours. Serve over noodles or rice.   *Makes 2 to 3 servings*

Barbara says: Serve beef tips over cooked noodles or rice.

peppered beef tips

city chicken bbq casserole

Jan Blue, Cuyahoga Falls, OH

    2 tablespoons vegetable oil
    6 to 8 boneless pork chops (about 2 pounds), cut into bite-size pieces
    ¼ cup chopped onions
    2 cloves garlic, chopped
    2 cups water
    2 cups uncooked instant rice
    2 cups (8 ounces) shredded mozzarella cheese

Sauce
    1 bottle (12 ounces) chili sauce
    1 cup ketchup
    ½ cup packed brown sugar
    2 tablespoons honey
    1 tablespoon Worcestershire sauce
    1 tablespoon hot pepper jelly
    1 teaspoon ground ginger
    1 teaspoon liquid smoke (optional)
    ½ teaspoon curry powder
    ¼ teaspoon black pepper

1. Preheat oven to 350°F.

2. Heat oil in large skillet over medium-high heat until hot. Add pork; cook and stir 10 to 15 minutes or until browned and barely pink in center. Add onions and garlic; cook until onions are tender. Drain fat.

3. Meanwhile, bring water to a boil in small saucepan. Stir in rice; cover. Remove from heat; let stand 5 minutes or until water is absorbed.

continued on page 56

city chicken bbq casserole

city chicken bbq casserole, continued

4. Combine sauce ingredients in separate saucepan; bring to a boil. Reduce heat to low; cover and simmer 10 minutes, stirring occasionally.

5. Combine pork mixture, rice and sauce in 2½-quart casserole; mix well. Bake 15 to 20 minutes. Top with mozzarella cheese and bake 5 minutes more. Serve hot. *Makes 6 to 8 servings*

Tip: "City chicken" is a traditional dish in Ohio and Pennsylvania. The name indicates that chicken was once more expensive than pork, so the cheaper pork cuts were prepared to taste like chicken.

rigatoni à la vodka

Jenni Smith, Feasterville, PA

>   1 pound ground beef
>   1 jar (26 ounces) pasta sauce
>   1½ cups 3-cheese pasta sauce
>   4 cups (16 ounces) shredded mozzarella and Cheddar cheese blend, divided
>   6 tablespoons vodka
>   12 ounces rigatoni pasta, cooked and drained

1. Preheat oven to 350°F. Spray 3-quart casserole with nonstick cooking spray. Cook beef in medium skillet over medium heat 5 minutes or until no longer pink, stirring to separate meat. Drain fat. Add pasta sauces, 2 cups cheese and vodka. Cook and stir until heated through.

2. Place cooked pasta in prepared casserole. Pour vodka sauce evenly over pasta; sprinkle with remaining 2 cups cheese.

3. Bake 15 minutes or until cheese has melted. *Makes 4 servings*

corned beef casserole

Barbara Gosen, Tucson, AZ

1 package (8 ounces) uncooked wide egg noodles
3 cups (12 ounces) shredded Mexican cheese blend, divided
1 can (12 ounces) corned beef
1 can (10¾ ounces) condensed cream of chicken or cream of mushroom soup, undiluted
1 cup milk
½ cup chopped onion
½ cup French fried onions

1. Preheat oven to 350°F.

2. Cook egg noodles according to package directions. Drain and keep warm.

3. Combine 2½ cups cheese, corned beef, soup, milk and chopped onion in large bowl. Add cooked noodles; mix well.

4. Transfer to 3- or 4-quart casserole; top with remaining ½ cup cheese. Sprinkle with French fried onions.

5. Bake, uncovered, 45 minutes or until hot and bubbly.   *Makes 6 to 8 servings*

round steak

Deborah Long, Bridgeport, CT

   1 boneless beef round steak (1½ pounds), trimmed and cut into 4 pieces
¼ cup all-purpose flour
   1 teaspoon black pepper
½ teaspoon salt
   1 tablespoon vegetable oil
   1 can (10¾ ounces) condensed cream of mushroom soup
¾ cup water
   1 medium onion, quartered
   1 can (4 ounces) sliced mushrooms, drained
¼ cup milk
   1 package (1 ounce) dry onion soup mix
      Salt
      Black pepper
      Ground sage
      Dried thyme leaves
   1 bay leaf

Slow Cooker Directions

1. Place steaks in large resealable plastic food storage bag. Close bag and pound with meat mallet to tenderize. Combine flour, 1 teaspoon black pepper and ½ teaspoon salt in small bowl; add to bag with steaks. Shake to coat meat evenly.

2. Heat oil in large nonstick skillet. Remove steaks from bag; shake off excess flour. Add steaks to skillet; brown on both sides.

3. Transfer steaks and pan juices to slow cooker. Add mushroom soup, water, onion, mushrooms, milk, dry soup mix, seasonings to taste and bay leaf to slow cooker; mix well. Cover; cook on LOW 5 to 6 hours or until steak is tender. Remove and discard bay leaf before serving.

Makes 4 servings

round steak

cantonese pork

Stacy Pineault, Mahwah, NJ

2 pork tenderloins (about 2 pounds)
1 tablespoon vegetable oil
1 can (8 ounces) pineapple chunks in juice, undrained
1 can (8 ounces) tomato sauce
2 cans (4 ounces each) sliced mushrooms, drained
1 medium onion, thinly sliced
3 tablespoons brown sugar
2 tablespoons Worcestershire sauce
1½ teaspoons salt
1½ teaspoons white vinegar
   Hot cooked rice

Slow Cooker Directions

1. Cut tenderloins in half lengthwise, then crosswise into ¼-inch slices. Heat oil in large nonstick skillet over medium-low heat. Brown pork on all sides. Drain excess fat; discard.

2. Place pork and remaining ingredients in slow cooker. Cover; cook on HIGH 4 hours or on LOW 6 to 8 hours. Serve over rice. *Makes 8 servings*

cantonese pork

jambalaya

Denise J. Dempsey, Farmington, MO

     1 pound ground beef
     1 cup chopped onion
    ¼ cup diced green bell pepper
     1 can (28 ounces) tomatoes, liquid drained and reserved
     1 teaspoon salt
    ½ teaspoon sugar
    ¼ teaspoon dried thyme leaves
     1 small bay leaf
    2⅓ cups cooked rice

1. Heat large skillet over medium heat. Add beef, onion and bell pepper; cook and stir until meat is no longer pink. Drain fat.

2. Add enough water to reserved tomato liquid to make 1½ cups. Add liquid, tomatoes, salt, sugar, thyme and bay leaf to skillet. Simmer 5 minutes.

3. Stir in rice; cover and simmer 5 minutes longer. Remove and discard bay leaf before serving.

Makes 4 to 6 servings

Helpful Hint: **If you prefer a spicier jambalaya, add hot pepper sauce just before serving.**

roast beef with mushrooms and vegetables

N.L. Banks, Hemet, CA

1 tablespoon vegetable oil
1 boneless beef chuck shoulder roast (3 to 5 pounds)
6 medium potatoes, peeled and halved
1 bag (1 pound) baby carrots
1 medium onion, quartered
1 can (10¾ ounces) condensed cream of mushroom soup
1 can (4 ounces) sliced mushrooms, drained
1 cup water

Slow Cooker Directions

1. Heat oil in large skillet over medium heat. Brown roast on all sides. Drain excess fat. Place roast in slow cooker. (If necessary, cut roast in half to fit in slow cooker.) Add potatoes, carrots and onion around roast.

2. Combine soup, mushrooms and water together in medium bowl. Pour over roast. Cover; cook on LOW 6 to 8 hours.

Makes 8 servings

smothered beef patties

Carol Occhipinti, Fort Worth, TX

Worcestershire sauce
Garlic powder
Salt
Black pepper
1 can (14½ ounces) Mexican-style diced tomatoes with chilies, undrained, divided
8 frozen beef patties, unthawed
1 onion, cut into 8 slices

Slow Cooker Directions

Sprinkle bottom of slow cooker with small amount of Worcestershire sauce, garlic powder, salt, pepper and 2 tablespoons tomatoes. Add 1 frozen beef patty. Top with Worcestershire, garlic powder, salt, pepper, 2 tablespoons tomatoes and 1 onion slice. Repeat layers. Cover; cook on LOW 8 hours.   *Makes 8 servings*

Carol says: Serve these patties with mashed potatoes and a Caesar salad. They are also delicious with steamed rice.

smothered beef patty

meat crust pie

Chris Gelinskey, Oconomowoc, WI

    1 pound ground beef
    2 cans (8 ounces each) tomato sauce, divided
    ½ cup seasoned dry bread crumbs
    ½ cup chopped green bell pepper, divided
    ¼ cup minced onion
    1 teaspoon salt, divided
    ⅛ teaspoon dried oregano leaves
    ⅛ teaspoon black pepper
    1 cup water
 1⅓ cups instant rice
    1 cup (4 ounces) grated Cheddar cheese, divided

1. Preheat oven to 350°F. Combine beef, ½ cup tomato sauce, bread crumbs, ¼ cup bell pepper, onion, ½ teaspoon salt, oregano and pepper in large bowl; mix well. Pat onto bottom and side of ungreased 9-inch deep-dish pie plate.

2. Bring water and remaining ½ teaspoon salt to boil in medium saucepan. Stir in rice; cover and remove from heat. Let stand 5 minutes or until water is absorbed. Add remaining 1½ cups tomato sauce, ½ cup cheese and remaining ¼ cup bell pepper to rice and mix well. Spoon rice mixture into meat shell. Cover with foil and bake 25 minutes.

3. Remove from oven and drain fat carefully, holding pan lid over pie to keep it from sliding. Top with remaining ½ cup cheese and return to oven. Bake, uncovered, 10 to 15 minutes or until cheese melts. Carefully drain fat again. Cut into wedges to serve. *Makes 6 to 8 servings*

meat crust pie

honey-baked heaven

Yuki Mountjoy, Des Moines, WA

    8 large Granny Smith apples (or other tart apples), peeled and sliced
    2 packages (8 ounces each) kielbasa sausage, cut into ½-inch slices
 1⅓ cups honey
    4 tablespoons water
    1 tablespoon ground cinnamon
 ⅓ cup butter

1. Preheat oven to 350°F.

2. Butter 13×9-inch baking dish. Arrange apples and sausage in baking dish.

3. Combine honey, water and cinnamon in medium bowl; mix well. Pour over apples and sausage. Dot with butter.

4. Bake 40 minutes, basting with pan juices occasionally, until apples are softened.

Makes 5 main-dish or 8 side-dish servings

michigan goulash

Diane Nemitz, Ludington, MI

2 tablespoons vegetable oil
1 pound ground beef or ground turkey
1 medium onion, chopped
1 large green bell pepper, seeded and diced
3 ribs celery, cut into thin slices
1 small zucchini, cut into slices
1 jalapeño pepper,* seeded and minced
1 can (8 ounces) tomato sauce
1 cup water
¾ cup barbecue sauce
1 package (8 to 10 ounces) noodles, cooked and kept warm
2 cups (8 ounces) shredded Cheddar cheese

Jalapeño peppers can sting and irritate the skin; wear rubber gloves when handling peppers and do not touch the eyes. Wash hands after handling.

1. Preheat oven to 350°F. Grease 13×9-inch baking dish.

2. Heat oil in large skillet over medium-high heat. Add beef, stirring to break up meat. Add onion, bell pepper, celery, zucchini and jalapeño pepper; cook and stir until meat is no longer pink. Add tomato sauce, water and barbecue sauce; stir to combine. Reduce heat to medium-low and simmer 20 minutes.

3. Combine meat mixture and noodles in prepared dish; top with cheese.

4. Bake 10 to 15 minutes or until cheese melts.

Makes 8 servings

cousin arlene's spaghetti lasagna

Arlene Vanderbilt, Palos Heights, IL

8 ounces uncooked spaghetti or other thin pasta
1 tablespoon butter
1 clove garlic, finely chopped
2 pounds 90% lean ground beef
1 teaspoon sugar
   Salt and black pepper
2 cans (8 ounces each) tomato sauce
1 can (6 ounces) tomato paste
1 cup (8 ounces) sour cream
1 package (3 ounces) cream cheese, softened
6 green onions, chopped
¼ cup grated Parmesan cheese

1. Preheat oven to 350°F. Cook spaghetti according to package directions until al dente. Drain; set aside.

2. Meanwhile, melt butter in large skillet over medium heat. Add garlic; cook and stir 1 minute. Add ground beef and sugar; season with salt and pepper. Cook and stir until beef is no longer pink; drain fat. Add tomato sauce and tomato paste; simmer 20 minutes, stirring occasionally.

3. Blend sour cream and cream cheese in medium bowl until smooth. Add green onions; mix well.

4. Spread a little meat sauce in 2-quart casserole. Layer ½ spaghetti, ½ sour cream mixture and ½ meat mixture. Repeat layers. Sprinkle with Parmesan cheese. Bake 35 minutes or until heated through.

Makes 6 servings

Arlene says: This casserole can be frozen; however, thaw it in the refrigerator overnight and bake until heated through.

cousin arlene's spaghetti lasagna

pastitsio

Marilyn Pocius, Oak Park, IL

    8 ounces uncooked ziti or elbow macaroni
    1 pound ground lamb or beef
    ½ cup chopped onion
    1 clove garlic, finely chopped
    1 can (about 8 ounces) tomato sauce
    ½ teaspoon dried oregano leaves
    ½ teaspoon black pepper
    ¼ teaspoon ground cinnamon
    2 tablespoons butter
    2 tablespoons all-purpose flour
  1½ cups milk
    1 egg, beaten
    1 cup grated Parmesan cheese, divided

1. Preheat oven to 350°F. Spray 9-inch baking dish with nonstick cooking spray.

2. Cook pasta according to package directions. Drain and reserve.

3. Cook and stir lamb, onion and garlic in large skillet over medium-high heat until lamb is no longer pink; drain fat. Stir in tomato sauce, oregano, pepper and cinnamon. Reduce heat to low and simmer 10 minutes.

4. Layer ½ of pasta in prepared baking dish. Top with meat mixture, then remaining pasta.

5. For sauce, melt butter in medium saucepan. Stir in flour. Cook and stir 1 minute. Whisk in milk. Cook, stirring constantly until thickened, about 6 minutes. Place beaten egg in small bowl; stir some of sauce into egg. Return egg mixture to saucepan; cook and stir 2 minutes. Stir in ¾ cup Parmesan cheese.

6. Pour sauce mixture over pasta layer. Sprinkle with remaining ¼ cup Parmesan. Bake 30 to 40 minutes until heated through and golden brown. *Makes 6 servings*

pastitsio

peking pork chops

Lynda McCormick, Burkburnett, TX

   6 pork chops, about 1 inch thick
   ½ cup soy or teriyaki sauce
   ¼ cup brown sugar
   ¼ cup Chinese ketchup or ketchup
   1 teaspoon ground ginger
   1 to 2 cloves garlic, crushed
      Salt
      Black pepper

Slow Cooker Directions

1. Trim excess fat from pork chops. Place chops in slow cooker.

2. Combine soy sauce, brown sugar, ketchup, ginger and garlic in small bowl; pour over meat. Cover; cook on LOW 4 to 6 hours or until pork is tender. Season with salt and pepper, if desired.

Makes 6 servings

Lynda says: Serve with steamed white rice (I prefer jasmine or sticky rice) and crisp Chinese noodles.

buck county ribs

Leonard Cranston, Westland, MI

4 boneless pork country-style ribs
1 teaspoon salt
1 jar (about 28 ounces) sauerkraut, drained
1 medium apple, diced
1 tablespoon sugar
1 teaspoon chicken bouillon granules *or* 1 cup chicken broth
    Mashed potatoes (optional)

Slow Cooker Directions

1. Place ribs in slow cooker. Sprinkle with salt.

2. Spoon sauerkraut over ribs. Top with apple. Sprinkle sugar over apple. Add bouillon granules. Cover; cook on LOW 8 to 9 hours. Serve with mashed potatoes, if desired.   *Makes 4 servings*

Helpful Hint: **Slow cooker recipes often provide a range of cooking times to account for variables such as the temperature of ingredients before cooking, the quantity of food in the slow cooker and the altitude.**

POULTRY FAVORITES

escalloped chicken

Billie Olofson, Des Moines, IA

  10 slices white bread, cubed
1½ cups cracker or dry bread crumbs, divided
   4 cups cubed cooked chicken
   3 cups chicken broth
   1 cup chopped onion
   1 cup chopped celery
   1 can (8 ounces) sliced mushrooms, drained
   1 jar (about 4 ounces) pimientos, diced
   3 eggs, lightly beaten
     Salt and black pepper
   1 tablespoon margarine

1. Preheat oven to 350°F.

2. Combine bread cubes and 1 cup cracker crumbs in large mixing bowl. Add chicken, broth, onion, celery, mushrooms, pimientos and eggs; mix well. Season with salt and pepper; spoon into 2½-quart casserole.

3. Melt margarine in small saucepan. Add remaining ½ cup cracker crumbs and brown, stirring occasionally. Sprinkle crumbs over casserole.

4. Bake 1 hour or until hot and bubbly.

Makes 6 servings

escalloped chicken

french country slow cooker chicken

Teri Lindquist, Gurnee, IL

1 medium onion, chopped
4 carrots, cut into ¼-inch slices
4 ribs celery, cut into slices
6 to 8 boneless skinless chicken breasts (about 1½ to 2 pounds)
1 teaspoon dried tarragon leaves
1 teaspoon dried thyme leaves
  Salt
  Black pepper
1 can (10¾ ounces) condensed cream of chicken soup, undiluted
1 envelope (1 ounce) dry onion soup mix
⅓ cup white wine or apple juice
2 tablespoons cornstarch
  Hot cooked rice (optional)

Slow Cooker Directions

1. Place onion, carrots and celery in slow cooker. Arrange chicken over vegetables. Sprinkle with tarragon, thyme, salt and pepper.

2. Pour condensed soup over chicken. Sprinkle with dry soup mix. Cover; cook on HIGH 3 to 4 hours, stirring once during cooking.

3. Twenty minutes before serving, whisk together wine and cornstarch in small bowl until smooth. Pour mixture over chicken; stir well. Cook, uncovered, on HIGH 15 minutes or until sauce thickens. Serve over rice, if desired. *Makes 6 to 8 servings*

french country slow cooker chicken

chicken stew

Terri Murr, Roanoke, AL

4 to 5 cups chopped cooked chicken
1 can (28 ounces) whole tomatoes, undrained
2 large potatoes, cut into 1-inch pieces
1 large onion, chopped
½ pound okra, sliced
1 can (14 ounces) cream-style corn
½ cup ketchup
½ cup barbecue sauce

Slow Cooker Directions

1. Combine chicken, tomatoes with juice, potatoes, onion and okra in slow cooker. Cover; cook on LOW 6 to 8 hours or until potatoes are tender.

2. Add corn, ketchup and barbecue sauce. Cover; cook on HIGH 30 minutes.

Makes 6 servings

Terri says: Serve this stew with hot crusty rolls and a green salad, and your meal is complete.

Helpful Hint: **To prepare fresh okra, rinse it under cold running water. Trim off and discard the stem ends. Cut the okra crosswise into ¹/₂- to 1-inch-wide slices. Okra's natural gumminess makes it a good thickener for soups and stews.**

penne chicken casserole

Yuki Mountjoy, Des Moines, WA

1½ pounds boneless skinless chicken breasts
3 cups water
2 cubes beef bouillon
4 cups cooked penne pasta
1 can (10¾ ounces) condensed cream of chicken soup, undiluted
1 cup sour cream
½ cup grated Asiago cheese
½ cup mayonnaise
⅓ cup dry sherry
½ cup dry Italian-seasoned bread crumbs
¼ cup grated Parmesan cheese
¼ cup margarine or butter, melted

1. Preheat oven to 350°F. Spray 2-quart casserole with nonstick cooking spray. Place chicken, water and bouillon cubes in large saucepan over medium heat. Cook 20 minutes or until chicken is no longer pink in center. Drain liquid and discard; cut chicken into cubes. Combine pasta and chicken in prepared casserole.

2. Combine soup, sour cream, Asiago cheese, mayonnaise and sherry in medium bowl; mix well. Spoon evenly over pasta and chicken.

3. Toss bread crumbs, Parmesan cheese and margarine in small bowl. Sprinkle over casserole. Bake 30 to 45 minutes or until top is golden brown. *Makes 6 servings*

chicken, asparagus & mushroom bake

Marilyn Pocius, Oak Park, IL

1 tablespoon butter
1 tablespoon olive oil
2 boneless skinless chicken breasts (about ½ pound), cut into bite-size pieces
2 cloves garlic, minced
2 cups sliced asparagus
1 cup mushroom slices
   Freshly ground black pepper
1 package (about 6 ounces) cornbread stuffing mix
¼ cup white wine (optional)
1 can (about 14 ounces) reduced-sodium chicken broth
1 can (10¾ ounces) low-sodium cream of asparagus or cream of chicken soup, undiluted

1. Preheat oven to 350°F. Heat butter and oil in large skillet. Cook and stir chicken and garlic about 3 minutes over medium-high heat until chicken is no longer pink. Add mushrooms, cook and stir 2 minutes more. Add asparagus; cook and stir about five minutes until vegetables soften slightly. Season with pepper.

2. Transfer mixture to 2½-quart casserole or six small casseroles. Top with stuffing mix.

3. Add wine to skillet, if desired; cook and stir 1 minute over medium-high heat, scraping up any browned bits from bottom of skillet. Add soup and broth; cook and stir until combined.

4. Pour soup mixture into casserole; mix well. Bake, uncovered, about 35 minutes (30 minutes for small casseroles) or until heated through and lightly browned. *Makes 6 servings*

Marilyn says: This is a good way to stretch a little leftover chicken into an easy and tasty dinner.

chicken, asparagus & mushroom bake

heidi's chicken supreme

Kim Adams, Manchester, MO

1 can (10¾ ounces) condensed cream of chicken soup, undiluted
1 package (1 ounce) dry onion soup mix
6 boneless skinless chicken breasts (about 1½ pounds)
½ cup imitation bacon bits *or* ½ pound bacon, crisp-cooked and crumbled
1 container (16 ounces) reduced-fat sour cream

Slow Cooker Directions

1. Spray slow cooker with nonstick cooking spray. Combine canned soup with dry soup mix in medium bowl; mix well.

2. Layer chicken breasts and soup mixture in slow cooker. Sprinkle with bacon bits. Cover; cook on HIGH 4 hours or on LOW 8 hours. During last hour of cooking, stir in sour cream.

Makes 6 servings

Kim says: This is delicious over noodles. You can also use condensed cream of mushroom or condensed cream of celery soup, if that is what you have on hand.

heidi's chicken supreme

turkey spaghetti sauce

Sandra Glasson, Flushing, MI

1 tablespoon vegetable oil
2 pounds ground turkey
1 can (12 ounces) beer
1 jar (26 ounces) spaghetti sauce
　Water
1 can (6 ounces) tomato paste
1 package (1½ ounces) dry spaghetti sauce seasoning mix

Slow Cooker Directions

1. Heat oil in large skillet over medium-low heat. Add turkey; cook and stir until turkey is no longer pink. Add beer; cook and stir 2 to 3 minutes or until mixture is well combined.

2. Place turkey mixture in slow cooker. Add spaghetti sauce. Fill empty sauce jar with water. Pour water into slow cooker. Add tomato paste and seasoning mix; stir to combine. Cover; cook on LOW 6 to 8 hours.

Makes 8 servings

Sandra says: I make this before I leave for work in the morning, and my children stir it when they get home from school. Then, when I get home from work, it's done!

chicken in honey sauce

Carol Wright, Cartersville, GA

4 to 6 boneless skinless chicken breasts
Salt
Black pepper
2 cups honey
1 cup soy sauce
½ cup ketchup
¼ cup oil
2 cloves garlic, minced
Sesame seeds

Slow Cooker Directions

1. Place chicken in slow cooker; sprinkle with salt and pepper to taste.

2. Combine honey, soy sauce, ketchup, oil and garlic in large bowl. Pour over chicken. Cover; cook on LOW 6 to 8 hours or on HIGH 3 to 4 hours.

3. Garnish with sesame seeds before serving.

Makes 4 to 6 servings

spicy shredded chicken

Amanda Neelley, Spring Hill, TN

6 boneless skinless chicken breasts (about 1½ pounds)
1 jar (16 ounces) prepared salsa

Slow Cooker Directions

Place chicken in slow cooker. Cover with salsa. Cover; cook on LOW 6 to 8 hours. Shred chicken with two forks before serving.   *Makes 6 servings*

Amanda says: Serve on warm flour tortillas with taco fixings.

slow cooker turkey breast

Bonnie Vezdos, Avon, OH

1 turkey breast (3 to 6 pounds)
  Garlic powder
  Paprika
  Dried parsley flakes

Slow Cooker Directions

Place turkey in slow cooker. Sprinkle with garlic powder, paprika and parsley to taste. Cover; cook on LOW 6 to 8 hours.   *Makes 6 servings*

Bonnie says: Don't add any liquid. The turkey makes its own juices.

spicy shredded chicken

chicken divan casserole

Susan Richardson, Libertyville, IL

1 cup uncooked rice
1 cup coarsely shredded carrots*
  Nonstick cooking spray
4 boneless skinless chicken breasts
2 tablespoons butter or margarine
3 tablespoons all-purpose flour
¼ teaspoon salt
  Black pepper
1 cup fat-free chicken broth
½ cup milk or half-and-half
¼ cup white wine
⅓ cup plus 2 tablespoons grated Parmesan cheese, divided
1 pound frozen broccoli florets

Coarsely shredded carrots are available in the produce section of many large supermarkets or shred them on a hand-held grater.

1. Preheat oven to 350°F. Lightly grease 12×8-inch baking dish.

2. Cook rice according to package directions. Stir in carrots. Spread mixture into prepared baking dish.

3. Spray large skillet with cooking spray. Heat over medium-high heat. Brown chicken breasts about 2 minutes on each side. Arrange over rice.

4. To prepare sauce, melt butter in 2-quart saucepan over medium heat. Whisk in flour, salt and pepper to taste; cook and stir 1 minute. Slowly whisk in broth and milk. Cook and stir until mixture comes to a boil. Reduce heat; simmer for 2 minutes. Stir in wine. Remove from heat. Stir in ⅓ cup cheese.

continued on page 92

chicken divan casserole

chicken divan casserole, continued

5. Arrange broccoli around chicken. Pour sauce over chicken and broccoli. Sprinkle remaining 2 tablespoons cheese over chicken.

6. Cover with foil; bake 30 minutes. Remove foil. Bake 10 to 15 minutes or until chicken is no longer pink in center and broccoli is hot.

Makes 6 servings

chicken reuben

Christine Haney, Valley View, OH

> 1 tablespoon butter or margarine
> 2 large sweet onions (preferably Vidalia), chopped
> 4 to 6 chicken breasts
> 1 jar (28 ounces) sauerkraut, drained
> 4 to 6 slices Swiss cheese
> 1 bottle (16 ounces) Thousand Island salad dressing

Slow Cooker Directions

1. Heat butter in large skillet over medium-low heat. Add onion and cook until tender.

2. Place half of chicken breasts in slow cooker. Top with half of onion mixture, half of sauerkraut, half of cheese slices and half of salad dressing. Repeat layers. Cover; cook on LOW 6 to 8 hours.

Makes 4 to 6 servings

Christine says: This recipe is outstanding—you're going to love it.

carmel chicken fresco bake

Elaine Sweet, Dallas, TX

    4 cups broccoli florets
    4 tablespoons butter, divided
  12 ounces baby portobello mushrooms, sliced
    3 shallots, diced
    1 can (14 ounces) artichoke hearts, rinsed, drained and quartered
    4 tablespoons all-purpose flour
2½ cups chicken broth
    1 teaspoon Dijon mustard
  ½ teaspoon salt
  ½ teaspoon dried tarragon leaves
  ½ teaspoon black pepper
    1 cup (4 ounces) shredded Emmentaler cheese
    2 pounds boneless skinless chicken breasts, cooked and cut into 1½-inch cubes
  ¼ cup grated Asiago cheese

1. Preheat oven to 350°F. Spray 4-quart baking dish with nonstick cooking spray; set aside.

2. Steam broccoli about 6 minutes or until tender. Rinse and drain under cold water. Set aside.

3. Melt 1 tablespoon butter in medium skillet over medium heat. Cook and stir mushrooms and shallots 5 minutes or until soft. Combine with broccoli in large bowl. Stir in artichoke hearts.

4. Melt remaining 3 tablespoons butter in same skillet. Blend in flour. Add chicken broth, mustard, salt, tarragon and pepper; whisk about 2 minutes or until sauce thickens. Add Emmentaler cheese and stir until smooth.

5. Alternately layer chicken and vegetable mixture in baking dish. Pour cheese sauce over top of casserole. Cover with foil and bake 40 minutes. Remove foil; sprinkle with Asiago cheese. Bake 5 to 10 minutes.

Makes 8 servings

saffron chicken & vegetables

Brenda Melancon, Bay St. Louis, MS

2 tablespoons vegetable oil
6 bone-in chicken thighs, skinned
1 bag (16 ounces) frozen mixed vegetables, such as broccoli, red peppers, mushrooms and onions,
  thawed
1 can (14½ ounces) roasted garlic flavor chicken broth
1 can (10¾ ounces) condensed cream of chicken soup, undiluted
1 can (10¾ ounces) condensed cream of mushroom soup, undiluted
1 package (about 8 ounces) saffron yellow rice mix with seasonings
½ cup water
½ teaspoon salt
1 teaspoon paprika (optional)

1. Preheat oven to 350°F. Spray 3-quart casserole with nonstick cooking spray; set aside.

2. Heat oil in large skillet over medium heat. Add chicken and brown well, about 10 minutes; drain fat.

3. Meanwhile, combine vegetables, chicken broth, soups, rice mix with seasonings, water and salt in large bowl. Place mixture in prepared casserole. Top with chicken. Sprinkle with paprika, if desired. Cover and bake 1½ hours or until chicken is no longer pink in the center.

Makes 6 servings

saffron chicken & vegetables

hot & sour chicken

Lynda McCormick, Burkburnett, TX

> 4 to 6 boneless skinless chicken breasts (about 1 to 1½ pounds)
> 1 package (1 ounce) dry hot-and-sour soup mix
> 1 cup chicken or vegetable broth

Slow Cooker Directions

Place chicken in slow cooker. Add soup mix and broth. Cover; cook on LOW 5 to 6 hours. Garnish as desired.

Makes 4 to 6 servings

Lynda says: This dish can be served over steamed white rice and topped with crispy Chinese noodles. Or, for a colorful variation, serve it over a bed of snow peas and sugar snap peas tossed with diced red bell pepper.

Helpful Hint: **Keep the lid on! The slow cooker can take as long as 30 minutes to regain heat lost when the cover is removed. Remove the cover only when instructed to do so in the recipe.**

hot & sour chicken

sunday dinner casserole

Ronda Tucker, Ten Mile, TN

2 cups sweet onion rings
½ cup cooking sherry
2 tablespoons sugar
2 tablespoons balsamic vinegar
1 teaspoon dried thyme leaves
½ teaspoon freshly ground black pepper
2 cups egg noodles, cooked and drained
2 pounds boneless skinless chicken breasts
3 cups chicken broth
1 can (14½ ounces) diced tomatoes, drained
2 cloves garlic, minced
½ teaspoon crushed red pepper
¼ cup chopped fresh basil
2 teaspoons grated lemon peel

1. Preheat oven to 400°F.

2. Combine onions, sherry, sugar, vinegar, thyme and black pepper in large skillet. Cook, stirring occasionally, over medium heat until onions begin to brown.

3. Meanwhile, place noodles in 13×9-inch baking dish. Top with chicken breasts.

4. Combine broth, tomatoes, garlic and red pepper with onions in skillet. Pour over chicken.

5. Bake, uncovered, 20 minutes; turn chicken breasts. Bake 20 to 25 minutes more or until chicken is no longer pink in center and juices run clear. Sprinkle with basil and lemon peel.

Makes 4 to 6 servings

gypsy's bbq chicken

Gypsy Heilman, Lawton, OK

6 boneless skinless chicken breasts (about 1½ pounds)
1 bottle (26 ounces) barbecue sauce
6 slices bacon
6 slices Swiss cheese

Slow Cooker Directions

1. Place chicken in slow cooker. Cover with barbecue sauce. Cover; cook on LOW 8 to 9 hours.

2. Before serving, cut bacon strips in half. Cook bacon in microwave or conventionally, keeping bacon flat.

3. Place 2 strips cooked bacon over each piece of chicken in slow cooker. Top with cheese slices. Cover; cook on HIGH until cheese melts.

Makes 6 servings

Gypsy says: If juices become too thick during cooking, add a little water.

Helpful Hint: **To microwave bacon, place bacon slices, without overlapping, in a single layer between paper towels on a plate. Microwave at HIGH for 45 seconds to 1 minute per slice.**

thyme for chicken stew with polenta dumplings

Diane Halferty, Corpus Christi, TX

2 pounds boneless skinless chicken thighs
4 tablespoons olive oil, divided
2 medium eggplants, chopped
6 small onions, chopped
4 tomatoes, seeded and diced
½ cup chicken broth
⅓ cup pitted black olives, sliced
1 tablespoon chopped fresh thyme *or* 1 teaspoon dried thyme leaves
1 tablespoon red wine vinegar
   Dumplings (recipe page 102)

1. Preheat oven to 350°F.

2. Rinse chicken; pat dry with paper towels. Heat 1 tablespoon oil over medium-high heat in 4-quart Dutch oven. Cook chicken in batches 4 to 5 minutes or until browned on all sides. Remove and set aside.

3. Heat remaining 3 tablespoons oil in same Dutch oven; add eggplant, onions and tomatoes. Reduce heat to medium. Cook, stirring occasionally, 5 minutes. Return chicken to Dutch oven. Add chicken broth, olives, thyme and vinegar; stir to combine. Bring to a boil. Transfer to oven; bake uncovered 1 hour. Meanwhile, prepare Dumplings.

4. Remove stew from oven; top with rounded tablespoonfuls dumpling mixture. Bake, uncovered, about 20 minutes or until dumplings are cooked through.   *Makes 6 servings*

continued on page 102

thyme for chicken stew with polenta dumplings

thyme for chicken stew with polenta dumplings, continued

Dumplings: Bring 3½ cups chicken broth to a boil in medium saucepan. Slowly whisk in 1 cup polenta or yellow cornmeal. Reduce heat to low; simmer, stirring constantly, 15 minutes or until thickened. Remove from heat; stir in 1 beaten egg, 2 tablespoons butter, ½ cup grated Parmesan cheese and ¼ cup chopped fresh parsley.

cheesy slow cooker chicken

Joan VandenNoven, Beloit, WI

> 6 boneless skinless chicken breasts (about 1½ pounds)
> Salt
> Black pepper
> Garlic powder
> 2 cans (10¾ ounces each) condensed cream of chicken soup, undiluted
> 1 can (10¾ ounces) condensed Cheddar cheese soup, undiluted
> Chopped fresh parsley (optional)

Slow Cooker Directions

1. Place 3 chicken breasts in slow cooker. Sprinkle with salt, pepper and garlic powder. Repeat with remaining 3 breasts.

2. Combine soups in medium bowl; pour over chicken. Cover; cook on LOW 6 to 8 hours. Garnish with parsley before serving, if desired.

Makes 6 servings

Joan says: The sauce is wonderful over noodles, rice or mashed potatoes.

cheesy slow cooker chicken

wild rice & chicken casserole

Andrée Tracey, St. Louis Park, MN

    1 package (6 ounces) long grain & wild rice mix
    2 tablespoons butter
    ½ cup chopped onion
    ½ cup chopped celery
    1 can (10¾-ounces) condensed cream of mushroom soup, undiluted
    ½ cup sour cream
    ⅓ cup dry white wine
    ½ teaspoon curry powder
    2 cups cubed cooked chicken

1. Preheat oven to 350°F.

2. Prepare rice mix according to package directions.

3. Meanwhile, melt butter in large skillet over medium heat; cook and stir onion and celery until tender. Stir in soup, sour cream, wine and curry powder.

4. Stir in chicken and rice. Transfer to 2-quart casserole. Bake 40 minutes or until heated through. Stir before serving.

Makes 4 to 6 servings

bonnie's slow-cooked turkey thighs with potatoes

Bonnie Luttrell, Bullhead City, AZ

1 large onion, cut into slices
2 turkey thighs, skin removed
2 cloves garlic, minced
½ teaspoon black pepper
8 to 10 small red potatoes
1 can (12 ounces) beer *or* 1½ cups chicken broth
1 can (8 ounces) tomato sauce
1 bay leaf

Slow Cooker Directions

1. Place onion slices in slow cooker. Arrange turkey thighs over onions; sprinkle with garlic and pepper.

2. Place potatoes around turkey thighs. Add beer, tomato sauce and bay leaf. Cover; cook on LOW 8 to 10 hours. Remove and discard bay leaf before serving.   *Makes 2 to 4 servings*

Bonnie says: The turkey will fall off the bones. It is great by itself or wrapped in tortillas.

chicken cassoulet

Marilyn Pocius, Oak Park, IL

    4 slices bacon
    ¼ cup all-purpose flour
       Salt and black pepper
 1¾ pounds chicken pieces
    2 cooked chicken sausages, cut into ¼-inch pieces
    1 onion, chopped
 1½ cups diced red and green bell pepper (2 small bell peppers)
    2 cloves garlic, finely chopped
    1 teaspoon dried thyme leaves
       Olive oil
       Salt and black pepper
    2 cans (about 15 ounces each) white beans, such as Great Northern, rinsed and drained
    ½ cup white wine (optional)

1. Preheat oven to 350°F. Cook bacon in large skillet over medium-high heat until crisp. Remove and drain on paper towels. Cut into 1-inch pieces.

2. Pour off all but 2 tablespoons fat from skillet. Combine flour, salt and black pepper in shallow bowl. Dip chicken pieces in flour; shake off excess. Brown chicken in batches over medium-high heat in skillet. Remove and set aside. Lightly brown sausages in same skillet. Remove and set aside.

3. Add onion, bell peppers, garlic, thyme, salt and black pepper to skillet. Cook and stir over medium heat about 5 minutes until softened. Add olive oil as needed to prevent sticking. Place in 13×9-inch baking dish. Add beans; mix well. Top with chicken, sausages and bacon. If desired, add wine to skillet; cook and stir over medium heat, scraping up brown bits. Pour over casserole.

4. Cover and bake 40 minutes. Uncover; bake 15 minutes more or until chicken is no longer pink in center.

Makes 6 servings

chicken cassoulet

slow cooker chicken and dressing

Shannon Athey, Bryn Mawr, PA

4 boneless skinless chicken breasts
   Salt and black pepper
4 slices Swiss cheese
1 can (14½ ounces) chicken broth
2 cans (10¾ ounces each) condensed cream of chicken, celery or mushroom soup, undiluted
3 cups packaged stuffing mix
½ cup butter, melted

Slow Cooker Directions

1. Place chicken in slow cooker. Season to taste with salt and pepper.

2. Top each breast with cheese slice. Add broth and soup. Sprinkle stuffing mix over top; pour melted butter over all. Cover; cook on LOW 6 to 8 hours or on HIGH 3 to 4 hours.

Makes 4 servings

Shannon says: This is one of our favorites!

my favorite chicken

MaryLou Rogers, Walla Walla, WA

    1 chicken (about 3 pounds), cut into pieces
    1 cup chopped onion
    1 cup sliced celery
    1 cup sliced carrots
    ½ teaspoon seasoned salt
    ½ teaspoon black pepper
    ¼ teaspoon garlic powder
    ¼ teaspoon poultry seasoning
    3 to 4 medium potatoes, cut into slices
    1 can (14 ounces) chicken broth

Slow Cooker Directions

Place chicken pieces, onion, celery, carrots, seasoning salt, black pepper, garlic powder and poultry seasoning in slow cooker. Top with potatoes. Pour broth over top. Cover; cook on HIGH 30 minutes. Reduce heat to LOW; cook 6 to 8 hours more. *Makes 4 servings*

MaryLou says: I put this on in the morning before work. We have a great dinner waiting for us when we get home in the afternoon. Using a slotted spoon, remove everything to a serving bowl. To thicken up the juices in the slow cooker, combine 1 tablespoon each cornstarch and water until smooth; stir into juices and cook until thickened. Pour over chicken mixture. It makes a great dinner!

SEAFOOD SENSATIONS

lemon shrimp

Aimee Dillman, Midlothian, IL

    1 package (12 ounces) uncooked egg noodles
    ½ cup (1 stick) butter, softened
    2 pounds cooked shrimp
    3 tomatoes, chopped
    1 cup chicken broth
    1 cup shredded carrots
    1 can (4 ounces) sliced mushrooms, drained
    2 tablespoons fresh lemon juice
    2 cloves garlic, chopped
    ½ teaspoon celery seed
    ¼ teaspoon black pepper

1. Preheat oven to 350°F.

2. Cook noodles according to package directions. Drain and mix with butter in large bowl, stirring until butter is melted and noodles are evenly coated. Add remaining ingredients and mix again. Transfer to 3-quart casserole.

3. Bake 15 to 20 minutes or until heated through.   *Makes 8 servings*

lemon shrimp

crab-artichoke casserole

Marilyn Pocius, Oak Park, IL

8 ounces uncooked small shell pasta
2 tablespoons butter
6 green onions, chopped
2 tablespoons all-purpose flour
1 cup half-and-half
1 teaspoon dry mustard
½ teaspoon ground red pepper
   Salt and black pepper
½ cup (2 ounces) shredded Swiss cheese, divided
1 package (about 8 ounces) imitation crabmeat chunks
1 can (about 14 ounces) artichoke hearts, drained and cut into bite-size pieces

1. Preheat oven to 350°F. Grease 2-quart casserole. Cook pasta according to package directions; drain and set aside.

2. Heat butter in large saucepan over medium heat; add green onions. Cook and stir about 2 minutes. Add flour; cook and stir 2 minutes more. Gradually add half-and-half, whisking constantly until mixture begins to thicken. Whisk in mustard, red pepper and season to taste with salt and black pepper. Remove from heat and stir in ¼ cup Swiss cheese until melted.

3. Combine crabmeat, artichokes and pasta in casserole. Add sauce mixture and stir well. Top with remaining ¼ cup cheese. Bake about 40 minutes until hot, bubbly and lightly browned.

Makes 6 servings

Marilyn says: This can also be baked in individual ovenproof dishes. Reduce cooking time to about 20 minutes.

crab-artichoke casserole

tuna tomato casserole

Cortney Morford, Tuckahoe, NJ

2 cans (6 ounces each) tuna, drained
1 cup mayonnaise
1 small onion, finely chopped
¼ teaspoon salt
¼ teaspoon black pepper
8 to 10 plum tomatoes, sliced ¼ inch thick
1 bag (12 ounces) uncooked wide egg noodles
1 cup (4 ounces) shredded Cheddar or mozzarella cheese

1. Preheat oven to 375°F.

2. Combine tuna, mayonnaise, onion, salt and pepper in medium bowl. Mix well and set aside.

3. Prepare noodles according to package directions, cooking just until tender. Drain noodles and return to pot.

4. Add tuna mixture to noodles; stir until well combined.

5. Layer half noodle mixture, half tomatoes and half cheese in 13×9-inch baking dish. Press down slightly. Repeat layers with remaining ingredients.

6. Bake 20 minutes or until cheese is melted and casserole is heated through.   *Makes 6 servings*

tuna tomato casserole

salmon casserole

Sandra Marie Swift, Pensacola, FL

2 tablespoons margarine or butter
2 cups mushroom slices
1½ cups chopped carrots
1 cup frozen peas
1 cup chopped celery
½ cup chopped onion
½ cup chopped red bell pepper
1 clove garlic, minced
1 teaspoon salt
½ teaspoon black pepper
1 tablespoon chopped fresh parsley
½ teaspoon dried basil leaves
4 cups cooked rice
1 can (14 ounces) red salmon, drained and flaked
1 can (10¾ ounces) condensed cream of mushroom soup, undiluted
2 cups (8 ounces) grated Cheddar or American cheese
½ cup sliced black olives

1. Preheat oven to 350°F. Spray 2-quart casserole with nonstick cooking spray; set aside.

2. Melt margarine in large skillet or Dutch oven over medium heat. Add mushrooms, carrots, peas, celery, onion, bell pepper, garlic, salt, black pepper, parsley and basil; cook and stir 10 minutes or until vegetables are tender. Add rice, salmon, soup and cheese; mix well.

3. Transfer to prepared casserole. Sprinkle olives over top. Bake 30 minutes or until hot and bubbly.

Makes 8 servings

salmon casserole

crab, shrimp & zucchini baked delight

Louise A. Donavant, Bellevue, WA

2 medium zucchini
1 cup flaked fresh crabmeat
1 cup small fresh bay shrimp
1 cup sour cream
⅓ cup sliced green pimento-stuffed olives
1 tablespoon finely chopped onion
1 tablespoon finely chopped green bell pepper
1 tablespoon fresh lemon juice
2 cups (8 ounces) shredded Cheddar cheese
   Paprika and parsley sprigs, for garnish (optional)

1. Preheat oven to 300°F. Butter 10×8-inch baking dish.

2. Place zucchini in saucepan of boiling water. Boil 3 to 5 minutes or until crisp-tender. Cool slightly. Cut each zucchini in half lengthwise. Scoop out seeds and some of flesh; discard seeds and flesh. Place in prepared baking dish, cut side up.

3. Combine crabmeat, shrimp, sour cream, olives, onion, bell pepper and lemon juice in large bowl; mix well. Place ¼ of crab mixture in each zucchini half. Top each zucchini half with ½ cup cheese.

4. Bake 1 hour or until lightly browned. Garnish with paprika and parsley sprigs, if desired.

Makes 4 servings

Note: This seafood filling can also be served as a salad. Garnish it with zucchini slices.

seafood pasta

Rita Berger, Wauconda, IL

½ cup olive oil
1 pound asparagus, cut into 1-inch pieces
1 cup chopped green onions
5 teaspoons chopped garlic
1 package (about 16 ounces) linguine, cooked and drained
1 pound medium shrimp, shelled, deveined and cooked
1 package (8 ounces) imitation crabmeat
1 package (8 ounces) imitation lobster
1 can (8 ounces) sliced black olives, drained

1. Preheat oven to 350°F. Spray 4-quart casserole with nonstick cooking spray. Heat oil in large skillet over medium heat. Cook and stir asparagus, green onions and garlic until tender.

2. Combine asparagus mixture, linguine, seafood and olives in prepared casserole. Bake 30 minutes or until heated through. *Makes 6 servings*

Helpful Hint: **Shrimp may be peeled and deveined either before or after they are cooked. If cooked, peel and devein them while they are still warm. The veins of medium shrimp are not gritty like those of large shrimp; removing the veins of medium or small shrimp is a personal preference.**

lickety-split paella pronto

Janice Elder, Charlotte, NC

1 tablespoon olive oil
1 large onion, chopped
2 cloves garlic, minced
1 jar (16 ounces) salsa
1 can (14½ ounces) diced tomatoes, undrained
1 can (14 ounces) artichoke hearts, drained and quartered
1 can (14 ounces) chicken broth
1 package (about 8 ounces) yellow rice
1 can (12 ounces) solid white tuna, drained and flaked
1 package (9 to 10 ounces) frozen green peas
2 tablespoons finely chopped green onions (optional)
2 tablespoons finely chopped red bell pepper (optional)

1. Heat oil in large nonstick skillet over medium heat until hot. Add onion and garlic; cook and stir about 5 minutes or until onion is tender.

2. Stir in salsa, tomatoes, artichokes, broth and rice. Bring to a boil. Cover; reduce heat to low and simmer 15 minutes.

3. Stir in tuna and peas. Cover; cook 5 to 10 minutes or until rice is tender and tuna and peas are heated through. Sprinkle each serving with green onions and red bell pepper, if desired.

Makes 4 to 6 servings

lickety-split paella pronto

shrimp creole

Marilyn Pocius, Oak Park, IL

2 tablespoons olive oil
1½ cups chopped green bell pepper
1 medium onion, chopped
⅔ cup chopped celery
2 cloves garlic, finely chopped
1 cup uncooked long grain rice
1 can (about 14 ounces) diced tomatoes, drained and juice reserved
1 teaspoon dried oregano leaves
¾ teaspoon salt
½ teaspoon dried thyme leaves
2 teaspoons hot pepper sauce, or to taste
Freshly ground black pepper
1 pound raw shrimp, peeled and deveined
1 tablespoon chopped fresh parsley (optional)

1. Preheat oven to 325°F. Heat olive oil in large skillet over medium-high heat. Add bell pepper, onion, celery and garlic; cook and stir 5 minutes or until vegetables are soft.

2. Add rice; cook and stir 5 minutes over medium heat until rice is coated. Add tomatoes, oregano, salt, thyme, hot pepper sauce and black pepper; stir to combine. Pour reserved juice into measuring cup. Add enough water to measure 1¾ cups liquid; add to skillet. Cook and stir 2 minutes.

3. Transfer mixture to 2½-quart casserole. Stir in shrimp. Bake, covered, 55 minutes or until rice is tender and liquid is absorbed. Sprinkle with parsley, if desired. *Makes 4 to 6 servings*

shrimp creole

cheesy tuna pie

Diane Nemitz, Ludington, MI

2 cups cooked rice
2 cans (6 ounces each) tuna, drained and flaked
1 cup mayonnaise
1 cup (4 ounces) shredded Cheddar cheese
½ cup sour cream
½ cup thinly sliced celery
1 can (4 ounces) sliced black olives
2 tablespoons onion flakes
1 refrigerated pie crust

1. Preheat oven to 350°F. Spray 9-inch, deep-dish pie pan with nonstick cooking spray.

2. Combine all ingredients except pie crust in medium bowl; mix well. Spoon into prepared pie pan. Place pie crust over tuna mixture; press edges to pie pan to seal. Cut slits for steam to escape.

3. Bake 20 minutes or until crust is browned and filling is bubbly.   *Makes 6 servings*

Diane says: This is super easy! It uses ingredients I always have on hand, and I love the made-from-scratch flavor.

cheesy tuna pie

seafood newburg casserole

Julie De Matteo, Clementon, NJ

1 can (10¾ ounces) condensed cream of shrimp soup, undiluted
½ cup half-and-half
1 tablespoon dry sherry
¼ teaspoon ground red pepper
3 cups cooked rice
2 cans (6 ounces each) lump crabmeat, drained
¼ pound medium shrimp, peeled and deveined
¼ pound bay scallops
1 jar (4 ounces) pimientos, drained and chopped
¼ cup finely chopped parsley

1. Preheat oven to 350°F. Spray 2½-quart casserole with nonstick cooking spray.

2. Whisk together soup, half-and-half, sherry and red pepper in large bowl until combined. Add rice, crabmeat, shrimp, scallops and pimientos; toss well.

3. Transfer to prepared casserole; sprinkle with parsley. Cover and bake about 25 minutes or until shrimp and scallops are opaque. *Makes 6 servings*

Helpful Hint: **To devein shrimp, cut a shallow slit along the back of the shrimp with a paring knife. Lift out the vein. You may find this easier to do under cold running water.**

seafood newburg casserole

GREAT SOUPS & CHILIS

1-2-3-4 chili

Carol Mason, Hanover Park, IL

> 2 pounds ground beef
> 4 cans (8 ounces each) tomato sauce
> 3 cans (15½ ounces each) chili beans in mild or spicy sauce, undrained
> Shredded Cheddar cheese (optional)
> Green onions, sliced (optional)

Slow Cooker Directions

1. Cook beef in large skillet over medium-high heat until no longer pink, stirring often to separate meat; drain fat.

2. Add beef, tomato sauce and beans to slow cooker; stir to mix well. Cover; cook on LOW 6 to 8 hours. Garnish with cheese and sliced green onions, if desired.   *Makes 8 servings*

Carol says: Just dump everything into your slow cooker. I set mine before I go to work, and get to come home to a batch of (cheater) chili! It tastes great with cornbread, too.

1-2-3-4 chili

chicken & barley soup

Susan Richardson, Libertyville, IL

1 cup thinly sliced celery
1 medium onion, coarsely chopped
1 carrot, cut into thin slices
½ cup medium pearled barley
1 clove garlic, minced
1 cut up whole chicken (about 3 pounds)
1 tablespoon olive oil
2½ cups chicken broth
1 can (about 14 ounces) diced tomatoes, undrained
¾ teaspoon salt
½ teaspoon dried basil leaves
¼ teaspoon black pepper

Slow Cooker Directions

1. Place celery, onion, carrot, barley and garlic in slow cooker.

2. Remove and discard skin from chicken pieces. Separate drumsticks from thighs. Trim back bone from breasts. Save wings for another use. Heat oil in large skillet over medium-high heat; brown chicken pieces on all sides. Place chicken in slow cooker.

3. Add broth, tomatoes with juice, salt, basil and pepper to slow cooker. Cook on LOW 7 to 8 hours or HIGH 4 hours or until chicken and barley are tender. Remove chicken from slow cooker; separate chicken from bones. Cut chicken into bite-size pieces, discarding bones; stir chicken into soup. *Makes 4 servings*

bobbie's vegetable hamburger soup

Jan Davis, Minneapolis, MN

1 teaspoon vegetable oil
1 pound extra-lean ground beef
2 cans (14½ ounces each) seasoned diced tomatoes, undrained
1 package (16 ounces) frozen vegetable blend
2 cups water
1 can (10¾ ounces) condensed tomato soup
1 envelope (1 ounce) dry onion soup mix
1 teaspoon sugar

Slow Cooker Directions

1. Heat oil in large skillet over medium-low heat. Cook beef until no longer pink. Drain excess fat.

2. Place ground beef and remaining ingredients in slow cooker; stir together. Cover; cook on LOW 6 to 8 hours.   *Makes 4 servings*

Bobbie says: Try this with ground turkey, too!

Helpful Hint: **Choose diced tomatoes seasoned with Italian herbs, basil or garlic for this easy soup.**

clam chowder

Karen Bassett, Citrus Heights, CA

> 5 cans (10¾ ounces each) condensed low-fat cream of potato soup, undiluted
> 2 cans (12 ounces each) evaporated skimmed milk
> 2 cans (10 ounces each) whole baby clams, rinsed and drained
> 1 can (14¾ ounces) cream-style corn
> 2 cans (4 ounces each) tiny shrimp, rinsed and drained
> ¾ cup crisp-cooked and crumbled bacon (about ½ pound) or imitation bacon bits
>   Lemon pepper to taste
>   Oyster crackers

Slow Cooker Directions

Combine all ingredients except crackers in slow cooker. Cover; cook on LOW 3 to 4 hours, stirring occasionally. Serve with oyster crackers.

Makes 10 servings

veggie soup with beef

Wanda Fortenberry, Elizabeth City, NC

> 1 pound beef stew meat
> 2 cans (15 ounces each) mixed vegetables
> 1 can (8 ounces) tomato sauce
> 2 cloves garlic, minced
>   Water

Slow Cooker Directions

Place all ingredients in slow cooker. Add enough water to fill slow cooker to within ½ inch of top. Cover; cook on LOW 8 to 10 hours.

Makes 4 servings

clam chowder

oven-baked black bean chili

Carolyn Blakemore, Fairmont, WV

1½ pounds lean ground beef
¼ cup chopped sweet onion
¼ cup chopped green bell pepper
1 can (about 15 ounces) black beans, rinsed and drained
1 can (14½ ounces) diced tomatoes with green chilies
1 can (about 14 ounces) beef broth
1 can (8 ounces) tomato sauce
5 tablespoons chili powder
1 tablespoon sugar
1 tablespoon ground cumin
1 teaspoon dried minced onion
⅛ teaspoon garlic powder
⅛ teaspoon ground ginger
2 cups (8 ounces) Mexican-blend shredded cheese

1. Preheat oven to 350°F. Cook and stir beef, onion and bell pepper in large skillet over medium-high heat until meat is no longer pink. Drain and transfer to 4-quart casserole.

2. Add remaining ingredients, except cheese; stir to combine. Cover and bake 30 minutes, stirring every 10 minutes or so. Uncover, top with cheese, and return to oven about 5 minutes or until cheese melts. *Makes 6 to 8 servings*

Carolyn says: This chili is great served with Mexican-style cornbread!

potato cheddar soup

Susan Richardson, Libertyville, IL

2 pounds red-skin potatoes, peeled and cut into ½-inch cubes
¾ cup coarsely chopped carrots
1 medium onion, coarsely chopped
3 cups chicken broth
½ teaspoon salt
1 cup half-and-half
¼ teaspoon black pepper
2 cups (8 ounces) shredded Cheddar cheese

Slow Cooker Directions

1. Place potatoes, carrots, onion, broth and salt in slow cooker. Cover; cook on LOW 6 to 7 hours or HIGH 3 to 3½ hours until vegetables are tender.

2. Stir in half-and-half and pepper; cover and cook on HIGH for 15 minutes. Turn off heat and remove cover; let stand 5 minutes. Stir in cheese until melted. *Makes 6 servings*

Susan says: I like to serve this soup topped with whole wheat croutons.

Helpful Hint: **Red-skin potatoes have a lower starch content and are good for use in soups. Round tan-skin potatoes may be substituted. Potatoes may be left unpeeled for this recipe, if you wish.**

hamburger soup

Scarlet Waxman, Orlando, FL

1 pound lean ground beef
1 package (1 ounce) dry onion soup mix
1 package (1 ounce) Italian salad dressing mix
¼ teaspoon seasoned salt
¼ teaspoon black pepper
3 cups boiling water
1 can (8 ounces) diced tomatoes, undrained
1 can (8 ounces) tomato sauce
1 tablespoon soy sauce
1 cup celery slices
1 cup thinly sliced carrots
2 cups cooked macaroni
¼ cup grated Parmesan cheese
2 tablespoons chopped fresh parsley

Slow Cooker Directions

1. Brown beef in medium skillet over medium-high heat; drain. Add beef, soup mix, salad dressing mix, seasoned salt and pepper to slow cooker. Stir in water, tomatoes with juice, tomato sauce and soy sauce. Add celery and carrots. Cover; cook on LOW 6 to 8 hours.

2. Increase heat to HIGH; stir in macaroni and Parmesan cheese. Cover; cook 10 to 15 minutes or until heated through. Sprinkle with parsley just before serving. *Makes 6 to 8 servings*

hamburger soup

shredded beef chili

Susan Hackitt, Tuscon, AZ

1 beef chuck shoulder roast (2 to 3 pounds)
1 can (15 ounces) corn, drained
1 can (4 ounces) diced green chilies
1 medium onion, diced
   Diced potatoes
   Chili powder

Slow Cooker Directions

1. Place roast, corn and chilies in slow cooker. Cover; cook on LOW 8 to 10 hours.

2. An hour before serving, remove roast and shred with 2 forks. Return meat to slow cooker. Add onion, potatoes and chili powder to taste. Cover; cook on HIGH 1 hour or until potatoes are tender. *Makes 6 to 8 servings*

Susan says: Top with Colby or Mexican cheese blend and serve either on flour tortillas or over rice. Serve refried beans, lettuce and tomato on the side, if desired.

simple hamburger soup

Gregg Sunderlin, Blairsville, PA

2 pounds ground beef or turkey, cooked and drained
1 can (28 ounces) whole tomatoes, undrained
2 cans (14 ounces each) beef broth
1 bag (10 ounces) frozen gumbo soup vegetables
½ cup uncooked pearl barley
1 teaspoon salt
1 teaspoon dried thyme leaves
   Black pepper

Slow Cooker Directions

1. Combine all ingredients in slow cooker. Add water to cover. Cover; cook on HIGH 3 to 4 hours or until barley and vegetables are tender.   *Makes 8 servings*

Gregg says: This is very easy to make. Try adding other frozen or canned vegetables or diced potatoes and carrots. Canned diced or stewed tomatoes can be substituted for the whole tomatoes. For a large crowd, add corn and serve with cornbread.

chili with chocolate

Shawna Steffen, Willmar, MN

    1 pound 95% lean ground beef sirloin
    1 medium onion, chopped
    3 cloves garlic, minced and divided
    1 can (28 ounces) diced tomatoes, undrained
    1 can (15½ ounces) chili beans in mild or spicy sauce, undrained
 1½ tablespoons chili powder
    1 tablespoon grated semisweet baking chocolate
 1½ teaspoons cumin
    ½ teaspoon salt
    ½ teaspoon black pepper
    ½ teaspoon hot pepper sauce

Slow Cooker Directions

1. Brown ground beef, onion and 1 clove garlic in large nonstick skillet over medium-low heat, stirring to break up meat; drain fat.

2. Place meat mixture in slow cooker. Add tomatoes with juice, beans, chili powder, remaining 2 cloves garlic, chocolate, cumin, salt, pepper and hot pepper sauce; mix well. Cover; cook on LOW 5 to 6 hours. Garnish as desired.   *Makes 4 servings*

chili with chocolate

A TASTE OF MEXICO

easy family burritos

Priss Lindsey, Albuquerque, NM

    1 beef chuck roast (2 to 3 pounds)
    1 jar (24 ounces) *or* 2 jars (16 ounces each) salsa
      Flour tortillas

Slow Cooker Directions

1. Place roast in slow cooker; top with salsa. Cover; cook on LOW 8 to 10 hours.

2. Remove meat from slow cooker. Shred with 2 forks. Return to slow cooker; cook 1 to 2 hours more. Serve shredded meat wrapped in warm tortillas. *Makes 8 servings*

Priss says: Garnish these burritos with any combination of ingredients such as shredded cheese, sour cream, salsa, lettuce, tomato, onion and guacamole. I sometimes make a batch of burrito meat and freeze it in family-size portions. It's quick and easy to reheat in the microwave on busy nights when there's no time to cook.

easy family burritos

cheesy chicken enchiladas

Julie DeMatteo, Clementon, NJ

4 tablespoons (½ stick) butter or margarine
1 cup chopped onion
2 cloves garlic, minced
¼ cup all-purpose flour
1 cup chicken broth
4 ounces cream cheese, softened
2 cups (8 ounces) shredded Mexican cheese blend, divided
1 cup shredded cooked chicken
1 can (7 ounces) chopped green chilies, drained
½ cup diced pimientos
6 (8-inch) flour tortillas, warmed
¼ cup chopped fresh cilantro
¾ cup prepared salsa

1. Preheat oven to 350°F. Spray 13×9-inch baking dish with nonstick cooking spray.

2. Melt butter in medium saucepan over medium heat. Add onion and garlic; cook and stir until onion is tender. Add flour, cook and stir 1 minute. Gradually whisk in chicken broth; cook and stir 2 to 3 minutes or until slightly thickened. Add cream cheese; stir until melted. Stir in ½ cup Mexican cheese blend, chicken, chilies and pimientos.

3. Spoon about ⅓ cup mixture onto each tortilla. Roll up and place, seam side down, in prepared baking dish. Pour remaining mixture over enchiladas; sprinkle with remaining 1½ cups Mexican cheese blend.

4. Bake 20 minutes or until bubbly and lightly browned. Sprinkle with cilantro and serve with salsa.

Makes 6 servings

cheesy chicken enchiladas

picadillo tamale casserole

Julie DeMatteo, Clementon, NJ

1½ pounds lean ground beef
1 cup chopped onion
2 cans (about 10 ounces each) diced tomatoes with green chilies, undrained
½ cup chicken broth
½ teaspoon ground cinnamon
6 tablespoons slivered almonds
6 tablespoons raisins
2 rolls (1 pound each) prepared polenta, cut into ½-inch-thick slices
2 cups (8 ounces) shredded Mexican cheese blend

1. Preheat oven to 350°F.

2. Cook and stir beef and onion in large skillet over medium heat for 5 minutes or until meat is no longer pink; drain fat.

3. Add tomatoes with juice, chicken broth and cinnamon; simmer 2 to 3 minutes. Stir in almonds and raisins.

4. Layer ½ of polenta slices, ½ of meat mixture and ½ of cheese in 13×9-inch casserole. Repeat layers.

5. Bake 25 to 30 minutes or until hot and bubbly.   *Makes 8 servings*

Helpful Hint: **Prepared polenta is available plain and in a variety of flavors. Look for rolls of this shelf-stable product in the ethnic food section of most large supermarkets.**

picadillo tamale casserole

zucornchile rajas bake

Elaine Sweet, Dallas, TX

    2 cups tomato sauce
    2 tablespoons chili powder
    2 tablespoons tomato paste
    1 tablespoon cider vinegar
    1 teaspoon ground cumin
    ½ teaspoon salt
    ½ teaspoon garlic powder
    ¼ teaspoon ground red pepper
    6 corn tortillas
      Vegetable oil for frying
    3 cups sliced zucchini
 1½ cups (6 ounces) shredded Monterey Jack or manchego cheese,* divided
    1 cup corn kernels
    1 can (4 ounces) diced green chilies, drained
    ½ to 1 cup sour cream
    3 green onions, chopped

Manchego cheese is a well-known Spanish cheese that melts easily. Look for it at specialty food markets.

1. Preheat oven to 350°F. Oil 13×9-inch baking dish.

2. Combine tomato sauce, chili powder, tomato paste, vinegar, cumin, salt, garlic powder and red pepper in medium saucepan. Bring to a boil over high heat; reduce heat to low and simmer 10 minutes, stirring occasionally.

3. Meanwhile, cut tortillas into ¼-inch-wide strips. Heat enough oil to cover bottom of medium skillet by ½ inch. Fry tortilla strips in batches until crisp; drain on paper towels.

4. Steam zucchini for 5 minutes; drain. Transfer to large bowl. Add ¾ cup cheese, corn, chilies and tortilla strips. Toss lightly to combine; spoon into prepared baking dish. Spread tomato sauce mixture over zucchini mixture and top with remaining ¾ cup cheese. Bake 30 minutes or until heated through.

5. Spread sour cream over top and sprinkle with green onions. Serve immediately.

Makes 6 to 8 servings

sandy's mexican chicken

Sandra Sebesta, Lockhart, TX

    2 to 4 chicken breasts
    1 medium onion, cut into strips
    1 can (10¾ ounces) condensed cream of chicken soup, undiluted
    1 can (10 ounces) Mexican-style tomatoes with green chilies, undrained
    1 package (8 ounces) processed cheese food, cubed

Slow Cooker Directions

1. Place all ingredients except cheese food in slow cooker. Cover; cook on LOW 6 to 8 hours or on HIGH 4 hours.

2. Break up chicken into pieces. Add cheese; cook on HIGH until melted.

Makes 2 to 4 servings

Sandra says: Serve over hot cooked spaghetti.

southwest spaghetti squash

Lynda McCormick, Burkburnett, TX

1 spaghetti squash (about 3 pounds)
1 can (about 14 ounces) Mexican-style diced tomatoes, undrained
1 can (about 14 ounces) black beans, rinsed and drained
¾ cup (3 ounces) shredded Monterey Jack cheese, divided
¼ cup finely chopped cilantro
1 teaspoon ground cumin
¼ teaspoon garlic salt
¼ teaspoon freshly ground black pepper

1. Preheat oven to 350°F. Cut squash in half lengthwise. Remove and discard seeds. Place squash, cut side down, in greased baking pan. Bake 45 minutes to 1 hour or until just tender. Using fork, remove spaghetti-like strands from hot squash and place strands in large bowl. (Use oven mitts to protect hands.)

2. Add tomatoes with juice, beans, ½ cup cheese, cilantro, cumin, garlic salt and pepper; toss well.

3. Spray 1½-quart casserole with nonstick cooking spray. Spoon mixture into casserole. Sprinkle with remaining ¼ cup cheese.

4. Bake, uncovered, 30 to 35 minutes or until heated through. Serve immediately.

Makes 4 servings

Lynda says: This is a very simple dish you can throw together in a few minutes, then bake. It's great for those nights you want to go meatless! And it's also a "kid-friendly" meal.

southwest spaghetti squash

cha-cha-cha casserole

Diane Halferty, Corpus Christi, TX

1 can (about 7 ounces) whole green chilies, drained
   Nonstick cooking spray
1 pound ground turkey or chicken
1 cup chopped onion
1 tablespoon chili powder or to taste
3 cloves garlic, minced
1 teaspoon ground cumin
1 teaspoon salt (optional)
1 can (10 ounces) diced tomatoes and green chilies, undrained
2 cups frozen corn, thawed, or 2 cups canned corn, drained
1 can (16 ounces) refried beans
2 cups (8 ounces) shredded Mexican cheese blend
2 cups crushed tortilla chips
1 cup seeded, diced fresh tomato
½ cup sliced green onions

1. Preheat oven to 375°F. Cut chilies in half lengthwise and arrange in single layer in 8-inch square baking dish coated with cooking spray.

2. Spray medium nonstick skillet with cooking spray. Cook and stir turkey, onion, chili powder, garlic, cumin and salt, if desired, over medium heat, until turkey is no longer pink. Add canned tomatoes with juice and cook about 10 minutes until liquid evaporates.

3. Add meat mixture to casserole; top with corn, then beans. Sprinkle with cheese and crushed chips. Bake for 30 minutes; let stand 5 minutes before serving. Garnish with fresh tomatoes and green onions. *Makes 6 servings*

cha-cha-cha casserole

green chili-chicken casserole

Lori Stokes, Odessa, TX

 4 cups shredded cooked chicken
1½ cups green enchilada sauce
 1 can (10¾ ounces) condensed cream of chicken soup, undiluted
 1 container (8 ounces) sour cream
 1 can (4 ounces) diced green chilies
 ½ cup vegetable oil
 12 (6-inch) corn tortillas
1½ cups (6 ounces) shredded Colby-Jack cheese, divided

1. Preheat oven to 325°F. Grease 13×9-inch casserole.

2. Combine chicken, enchilada sauce, soup, sour cream and chilies in large skillet over medium-high heat. Stir until warm.

3. Heat oil in separate deep skillet. Fry tortillas just until soft; drain on paper towels. Place 4 tortillas on bottom of prepared casserole. Layer with ⅓ chicken mixture and ½ cup cheese. Repeat layers twice.

4. Bake 15 to 20 minutes or until cheese is melted and casserole is heated through.

Makes 6 servings

Helpful Hint: **Shredded Mexican blend cheese may be substituted for the Colby-Jack cheese in this recipe.**

green chili-chicken casserole

mexican lasagna

Kay Butram, Aurora, OH

1 pound ground beef
1 envelope (about 1 ounce) taco seasoning
1 can (14½ ounces) Mexican-style diced tomatoes, undrained
1½ teaspoons chili powder
1 teaspoon ground cumin
½ teaspoon salt
½ teaspoon crushed red pepper
2 cups (16 ounces) sour cream
1 can (4 ounces) diced green chilies, drained
6 green onions, chopped
6 to 7 (8-inch) flour tortillas
1 can (15 ounces) corn, drained
2 cups (8 ounces) shredded Cheddar cheese

1. Preheat oven to 350°F. Grease 13×9-inch baking dish.

2. Cook and stir ground beef with taco seasoning in large skillet over medium heat until meat is no longer pink. Drain fat; set aside.

3. Combine tomatoes with juice, chili powder, cumin, salt and red pepper in medium bowl. Set aside.

4. Combine sour cream, chilies and green onions in separate small bowl.

5. Layer ⅓ of tomato mixture, 2 tortillas, ⅓ of sour cream mixture, ⅓ of meat mixture, ⅓ of corn and ⅓ of cheese in prepared casserole. Repeat layers twice.

6. Bake 35 minutes or until bubbly. Let stand 15 minutes before serving. Garnish with olives and additional green onions, if desired.

Makes 4 servings

taco salad casserole

Tammy Rose, Princeton, WV

1 pound ground beef
1 cup chopped onion
1 can (15 ounces) chili with beans
1 can (14½ ounces) diced tomatoes, undrained
1 can (4 ounces) chopped green chilies, undrained
1 package (about 1 ounce) taco seasoning mix
1 bag (12 ounces) nacho-flavor tortilla chips, crushed and divided
2 cups (8 ounces) shredded Cheddar cheese
2 cups (8 ounces) shredded mozzarella cheese
3 to 4 cups shredded lettuce
1 jar (8 ounces) prepared taco sauce
½ cup sour cream

1. Preheat oven to 350°F.

2. Cook and stir beef and onion in large skillet over medium heat until meat is no longer pink; drain fat. Add chili with beans, tomatoes with juice, green chilies and taco seasoning; cook and stir until heated through.

3. Place half of tortilla chips in 2½-quart casserole. Pour meat mixture over chips and top with cheeses and remaining chips. Bake 30 to 40 minutes or until hot and bubbly.

4. Serve over bed of lettuce; top with taco sauce and sour cream. *Makes 6 to 8 servings*

slow cooker stuffed peppers

Susan Ambrose, Cabot, PA

1 package (about 7 ounces) Spanish rice mix
1 pound ground beef
½ cup diced celery
1 small onion, chopped
1 egg, beaten
4 medium green bell peppers, halved lengthwise, cored and seeded
1 can (28 ounces) whole peeled tomatoes, undrained
1 can (10¾ ounces) condensed tomato soup
1 cup water

Slow Cooker Directions

1. Set aside seasoning packet from rice. Combine beef, rice mix, celery, onion and egg in large bowl. Divide meat mixture evenly among pepper halves.

2. Pour tomatoes with juice into slow cooker. Arrange filled pepper halves on top of tomatoes. Combine tomato soup, water and reserved rice mix seasoning packet in large bowl. Pour over peppers. Cover; cook on LOW 8 to 10 hours. *Makes 4 servings*

Helpful Hint: When buying bell peppers for stuffing, look for round, blocky ones that will stand up straight. If necessary, you can trim a little from the bottom of a bell pepper to make it level.

slow cooker stuffed pepper

esperanza's enchiladas

Linda S. Killion Scott, Santa Rosa, CA

     1 cup vegetable oil
    12 corn tortillas, cut into 1-inch pieces
    1½ to 2 pounds ground beef
     ⅓ cup finely chopped yellow onion
     1 can (10½ ounces) enchilada sauce
     1 can (8 ounces) tomato sauce
     ¼ cup water
     1 envelope (about 1 ounce) taco or enchilada seasoning mix
     2 cups (8 ounces) shredded mild Cheddar cheese
     2 cups (8 ounces) shredded Monterey Jack cheese
     1 can (6 ounces) black olives, drained and chopped
     6 green onions, finely chopped
       Sour cream (optional)
       Guacamole (optional)

1. Preheat oven to 350°F.

2. Heat oil in medium skillet over medium-high heat. Add enough tortilla pieces to fill, but not crowd the skillet; fry until crisp. Remove with slotted spoon; set aside to drain on paper towels. Repeat with remaining tortilla pieces.

3. Cook and stir ground beef and onion in large skillet over medium-high heat stirring to break up meat until beef is browned; drain fat. Add enchilada sauce, tomato sauce, water and taco seasoning mix. Bring to a boil over high heat. Reduce heat to low and simmer 20 minutes.

4. Combine beef mixture with ⅔ of fried tortilla pieces in large bowl; transfer to 13×9-inch baking dish. Top with remaining ⅓ of tortilla pieces, cheeses, olives and green onions. Bake until cheeses are melted, about 5 to 10 minutes. Garnish with sour cream and guacamole, if desired.

Makes 6 to 8 servings

esperanza's enchiladas

spicy chicken casserole with corn bread

Kathy Rouse, Fayetteville, NC

2 tablespoons olive oil
4 skinless boneless chicken breasts, cut into bite-size pieces
1 envelope (about 1 ounce) taco seasoning
1 can (about 15 ounces) black beans, rinsed and drained
1 can (14½ ounces) diced tomatoes, drained
1 can (about 10 ounces) Mexican-style corn, drained
1 can (about 4 ounces) diced chilies, drained
½ cup mild salsa
1 box (about 8½ ounces) corn bread mix, plus ingredients for mix
½ cup (2 ounces) shredded Cheddar cheese
¼ cup chopped red bell pepper

1. Heat oil in large skillet over medium heat. Cook chicken until no longer pink. Sprinkle taco seasoning over chicken. Add beans, tomatoes, corn, chilies and salsa; stir until well blended. Transfer to 2-quart casserole sprayed with nonstick cooking spray.

2. Prepare corn bread mix according to package directions, adding cheese and bell pepper. Pour over chicken mixture.

3. Bake at 350°F for 30 minutes or until corn bread is golden brown. *Makes 4 to 6 servings*

spicy chicken casserole with corn bread

A TASTE OF ITALY

eggplant parmigiana

Theresa Moreau, Utica, NY

  2 eggs, beaten
¼ cup milk
   Dash *each* of garlic powder, onion powder, salt and black pepper
  1 large eggplant, cut into ½-inch-thick slices
½ cup seasoned dry bread crumbs
   Vegetable oil for frying
  1 jar (about 26 ounces) spaghetti sauce
  4 cups (16 ounces) shredded mozzarella cheese
2½ cups (10 ounces) shredded Swiss cheese
¼ cup grated Parmesan cheese
¼ cup grated Romano cheese

1. Preheat oven to 350°F. Combine eggs, milk, garlic powder, onion powder, salt and pepper in shallow bowl. Dip eggplant in egg mixture and then coat in bread crumbs.

2. Add enough oil to large skillet to cover bottom by ¼ inch. Heat over medium-high heat. Brown eggplant in batches on both sides; drain on paper towels. Cover bottom of 13×9-inch baking dish with 3 tablespoons sauce. Layer half of eggplant, half of mozzarella cheese, half of Swiss cheese and half of remaining sauce in dish. Repeat layers. Sprinkle with Parmesan and Romano cheeses.

3. Bake 30 minutes or until heated through and cheeses are melted. *Makes 4 servings*

eggplant parmigiana

italian tomato bake

Terry Lunday, Flagstaff, AZ

1 pound sweet Italian sausage, cut into ½-inch slices
2 tablespoons margarine or butter
1 cup chopped onion
2 cups frozen broccoli florets
4 cups cooked egg noodles
2 cups prepared spaghetti sauce
½ cup diced tomatoes
2 cloves garlic, minced
3 plum tomatoes, sliced
1 cup (8 ounces) low-fat ricotta cheese
⅓ cup grated Parmesan cheese
1 teaspoon dried oregano leaves

1. Preheat oven to 350°F. Cook sausage in large skillet over medium heat about 10 minutes or until barely pink in center. Drain on paper towels; set aside. Drain fat from skillet.

2. Add margarine and onion to skillet; cook and stir until onion is tender. Meanwhile, steam broccoli 5 minutes until crisp-tender; drain. Combine onion mixture, noodles, spaghetti sauce, broccoli, diced tomatoes and garlic in large bowl; mix well.

3. Transfer to 13×9-inch baking dish. Top with sausage and arrange tomato slices over top. Place 1 heaping tablespoon ricotta cheese on each tomato slice. Sprinkle casserole with Parmesan cheese and oregano. Bake 35 minutes or until hot and bubbly.   *Makes 6 servings*

italian tomato bake

easy parmesan chicken

Susan Richardson, Libertyville, IL

8 ounces mushrooms, sliced
1 medium onion, cut in thin wedges
1 tablespoon olive oil
4 boneless skinless chicken breasts
1 jar (26 ounces) pasta sauce
½ teaspoon dried basil leaves
¼ teaspoon dried oregano leaves
1 bay leaf
½ cup (2 ounces) shredded part-skim mozzarella cheese
¼ cup grated Parmesan cheese
Hot cooked spaghetti (optional)

Slow Cooker Directions

1. Place mushrooms and onion in slow cooker.

2. Heat oil in large skillet over medium-high heat until hot. Lightly brown chicken on both sides. Place chicken in slow cooker. Pour pasta sauce over chicken; add herbs. Cook on HIGH 3 hours or on LOW 6 to 7 hours or until chicken is tender. Remove and discard bay leaf.

3. Sprinkle chicken with cheeses. Cook, uncovered, on LOW 15 to 30 minutes or until cheeses are melted. Serve over spaghetti, if desired. *Makes 4 servings*

Tip: Other vegetables, such as sliced zucchini, cubed eggplant or broccoli florets, can be substituted for the mushroom slices.

italian combo subs

Valorie Rowland, Hardin, KY

1 tablespoon vegetable oil
1 pound boneless beef round steak, cut into thin strips
1 pound bulk Italian sausage
1 green bell pepper, cut into strips
1 medium onion, thinly sliced
1 can (4 ounces) sliced mushrooms, drained (optional)
  Salt
  Black pepper
1 jar (26 ounces) spaghetti sauce
2 loaves Italian bread, cut into 1-inch-thick slices

Slow Cooker Directions

1. Heat oil in large skillet over medium-high heat. Brown meat on both sides. Drain and discard fat. Place meat in slow cooker.

2. In same skillet, cook and stir Italian sausage until no longer pink. Drain and discard fat. Add sausage to slow cooker.

3. Place bell pepper, onion and mushrooms, if desired, over meat in slow cooker. Season to taste with salt and black pepper. Top with spaghetti sauce. Cover; cook on LOW 4 to 6 hours. Serve mixture on bread. *Makes 6 servings*

Serving Suggestion: Top with freshly grated Parmesan cheese.

tuscan baked rigatoni

Julie DeMatteo, Clementon, NJ

1 pound Italian sausages, casings removed
1 pound rigatoni pasta, cooked, drained and kept warm
2 cups (8 ounces) shredded fontina cheese
2 tablespoons olive oil
2 fennel bulbs, thinly sliced
4 cloves garlic, minced
1 can (28 ounces) crushed tomatoes
1 cup heavy cream
1 teaspoon salt
1 teaspoon black pepper
8 cups coarsely chopped fresh spinach
1 can (15 ounces) cannellini beans, rinsed and drained
2 tablespoons pine nuts
½ cup grated Parmesan cheese

1. Preheat oven to 350°F. Spray 4-quart casserole with nonstick cooking spray. Crumble sausage in large skillet over medium-high heat. Cook and stir until no longer pink; drain. Transfer sausage to large bowl. Add pasta and fontina cheese; mix well.

2. Combine oil, fennel and garlic in same skillet. Cook and stir over medium heat 3 minutes or until fennel is tender. Add tomatoes, cream, salt and pepper; cook and stir until slightly thickened. Stir in spinach, beans and pine nuts; cook until heated through.

3. Pour sauce over pasta and sausage; toss to coat. Transfer to prepared casserole; sprinkle evenly with Parmesan cheese. Bake 30 minutes or until hot and bubbly. *Makes 6 to 8 servings*

tuscan baked rigatoni

pesto lasagna

Karen Jensen, Evanston, IL

1 package (16 ounces) lasagna noodles
3 tablespoons olive oil
1½ cups chopped onion
3 cloves garlic, finely chopped
3 packages (10 ounces each) frozen chopped spinach, thawed and squeezed dry
3 cups (24 ounces) ricotta cheese
1½ cups prepared pesto sauce
¾ cup grated Parmesan cheese
½ cup pine nuts, toasted
4 cups (16 ounces) shredded mozzarella cheese
Strips of roasted red pepper (optional)

1. Preheat oven to 350°F. Oil 13×9-inch casserole or lasagna pan. Partially cook lasagna noodles according to package directions.

2. Heat oil in large skillet. Cook and stir onion and garlic until transparent. Add spinach; cook and stir about 5 minutes. Season with salt and pepper. Transfer to large bowl.

3. Add ricotta cheese, pesto, Parmesan cheese and pine nuts to spinach mixture; mix well.

4. Layer 5 lasagna noodles, slightly overlapping, in prepared casserole. Top with ⅓ of spinach-ricotta mixture, and ⅓ of mozzarella. Repeat layers twice.

5. Bake about 35 minutes until hot and bubbly. Garnish with red pepper, if desired.

Makes 8 servings

pesto lasagna

italian pot roast
Jodi Castiglione, Chandler, AZ

    1 beef chuck shoulder roast (2 to 3 pounds)
    1 can (28 ounces) crushed tomatoes, undrained, *or* 6 to 8 fresh plum tomatoes, chopped
    1 package (1 ounce) dry spaghetti sauce seasoning mix
    1 teaspoon minced garlic *or* ½ teaspoon garlic powder
    1 teaspoon Italian seasoning
    1 package (16 ounces) spaghetti or other pasta, cooked according to package directions
    Grated Parmesan cheese

Slow Cooker Directions

Place all ingredients except spaghetti and cheese in slow cooker. Cover; cook on HIGH 5 to 6 hours. Serve sliced roast over hot cooked spaghetti. Sprinkle with Parmesan cheese.

Makes 6 to 8 servings

nice 'n' easy italian chicken
Marcia Szczepaniak, Williamsville, NY

    4 boneless skinless chicken breasts (about 1 pound)
    8 ounces mushrooms, sliced
    1 medium green bell pepper, chopped (optional)
    1 medium zucchini, diced
    1 medium onion, chopped
    1 jar (26 ounces) spaghetti sauce

Slow Cooker Directions

Combine all ingredients in slow cooker. Cover; cook on LOW 6 to 8 hours.

Makes 4 servings

nicole's favorite slow cooker chicken cacciatore

Jane Paquet, Unionville, CT

6 boneless skinless chicken breasts (about 1½ pounds)
   Garlic powder
   Onion powder
   Seasoned salt
   Italian seasoning
   Black pepper
10 ounces mushrooms, sliced
 1 can (15 ounces) Italian-style tomato sauce
¼ cup red wine or chicken broth
 8 ounces bow-tie pasta, cooked according to package directions

Slow Cooker Directions

1. Spray inside of slow cooker with nonstick cooking spray. Place chicken in slow cooker. Sprinkle generously with seasonings to taste.

2. Add mushrooms. Add tomato sauce and wine. Cover; cook on LOW 6 hours. Serve with hot cooked pasta.

Makes 6 servings

manicotti

Billie Olofson, Des Moines, IA

1 container (16 ounces) ricotta cheese
2 cups (8 ounces) shredded mozzarella cheese
½ cup cottage cheese
2 tablespoons grated Parmesan cheese
2 eggs, beaten
½ teaspoon minced garlic
Salt and black pepper
1 package (about 8 ounces) uncooked manicotti shells
1 pound ground beef
1 jar (26 ounces) spaghetti sauce
2 cups water

1. Combine ricotta cheese, mozzarella cheese, cottage cheese, Parmesan cheese, eggs and garlic in large bowl; mix well. Season with salt and pepper.

2. Stuff mixture into uncooked manicotti shells using narrow rubber spatula. Place filled shells in 13×9-inch baking dish. Preheat oven to 375°F.

3. Cook ground beef in large skillet over medium-high heat until no longer pink, stirring to separate. Drain off excess fat. Stir in spaghetti sauce and water (mixture will be thin). Pour sauce over filled manicotti shells.

4. Cover with foil; bake 1 hour or until sauce has thickened and shells are tender.

Makes 6 servings

manicotti

spicy italian beef

Barbara Mohrle, Dallas, TX

1 boneless beef chuck roast (3 to 4 pounds)
1 jar (12 ounces) peperoncini
1 can (14½ ounces) beef broth
1 can (12 ounces) beer
1 package (1 ounce) Italian salad dressing mix
1 loaf French bread, cut into thick slices
10 slices provolone cheese (optional)

Slow Cooker Directions

1. Trim fat from roast. Cut roast, if necessary, to fit in slow cooker, leaving meat in as many large pieces as possible.

2. Drain peppers; pull off stem ends and discard. Add peppers, broth, beer and dressing mix to slow cooker; *do not stir.* Cover; cook on LOW 8 to 10 hours.

3. Remove meat from slow cooker; shred with 2 forks. Return shredded meat to slow cooker; mix well. Serve on French bread, topped with cheese, if desired. Add additional sauce and peppers as desired.

Makes 8 to 10 servings

Helpful Hint: **Peperoncini are thin, 2- to 3-inch-long mild peppers that are pickled. Look for them in the Italian foods or pickled foods section of the supermarket.**

spicy italian beef

zucchini parmigiana casserole

Tanya Bates, Clearwater, FL

½ cup all-purpose flour
3 eggs, beaten
2 cups Italian-seasoned bread crumbs
6 cups zucchini slices
½ cup olive oil
1 pound lean ground beef
½ pound bulk sausage
1 cup chopped onion
1 tablespoon minced garlic
¼ cup chopped fresh basil
2 tablespoons chopped fresh oregano
4 cups tomato sauce
2 cups (8 ounces) shredded mozzarella
¼ cup grated Parmesan cheese
¼ cup chopped fresh parsley

1. Preheat oven to 350°F. Place flour, eggs and bread crumbs in separate shallow bowls. Dip zucchini in flour, egg, then bread crumbs to coat. Heat olive oil in medium skillet over medium-high heat. Brown zucchini on both sides in batches; season with salt and pepper. Drain zucchini on paper towels. Discard oil.

2. Add ground beef, sausage, onion and garlic to same skillet. Cook and stir until meat is no longer pink. Drain fat. Stir in basil and oregano.

3. Layer half of tomato sauce, half of zucchini, half of meat mixture, half of mozzarella and half of Parmesan in 4-quart casserole. Repeat layers.

4. Bake 30 minutes or until heated through and cheese is melted. Top with parsley.

Makes 6 servings

italian chicken my way

Debbie Auterson, Rio, CA

½ cup dry bread crumbs
¼ cup grated Parmesan cheese
6 boneless skinless chicken breasts, cut in half lengthwise
4 tablespoons (½ stick) margarine
1 package (10 ounces) frozen chopped broccoli, thawed
1 teaspoon garlic powder
1 teaspoon Italian seasoning
1 jar (26 ounces) spaghetti sauce
2 cups (8 ounces) shredded mozzarella cheese

1. Preheat oven to 350°F. Combine bread crumbs and Parmesan cheese in shallow bowl. Place chicken breast halves one at a time in bread crumb mixture, pressing to coat both sides.

2. Heat margarine in large skillet over medium-high heat. Cook chicken in batches until browned on both sides. Transfer chicken to 13×9-inch casserole coated with nonstick cooking spray. Top with broccoli; sprinkle with garlic powder and Italian seasoning. Cover with spaghetti sauce. Top with cheese.

3. Bake 25 minutes or until hot and bubbly and chicken is no longer pink in center.

Makes 12 servings

pizza casserole

Richard White, Lewistown, PA

    2 cups uncooked rotini or other spiral pasta
1½ to 2 pounds ground beef
    1 medium onion, chopped
      Salt and black pepper
    1 can (about 15 ounces) pizza sauce
    1 can (8 ounces) tomato sauce
    1 can (6 ounces) tomato paste
  ½ teaspoon sugar
  ½ teaspoon garlic salt
  ½ teaspoon dried oregano leaves
    2 cups (8 ounces) shredded mozzarella cheese
 12 to 15 slices pepperoni

1. Preheat oven to 350°F. Cook rotini according to package directions. Set aside.

2. Meanwhile, cook and stir ground beef and onion in large skillet over medium-high heat until meat is no longer pink. Season with salt and pepper. Set aside.

3. Combine rotini, pizza sauce, tomato sauce, tomato paste, sugar, garlic salt and oregano in large bowl. Add beef mixture and stir until blended.

4. Place half of mixture in 3-quart casserole; top with 1 cup cheese. Repeat layers. Arrange pepperoni slices on top. Bake 25 to 30 minutes or until heated through and cheese is melted.

Makes 6 servings

pizza casserole

BLUE-RIBBON SIDES

summer squash casserole

Darleen Presnell, Deep Gap, NC

  2 cups sliced yellow summer squash
  1 medium carrot, thinly sliced
  ½ cup chopped onion
  ½ cup diced red or green bell pepper
  ½ teaspoon salt
  ⅛ teaspoon black pepper
  1 can (10¾ ounces) condensed cream of chicken or mushroom soup, undiluted
  1 container (8 ounces) sour cream
  1 cup (4 ounces) shredded Italian cheese blend
  1 cup (4 ounces) shredded Cheddar cheese
  1 package (6 ounces) stuffing mix

1. Preheat oven to 350°F. Combine squash, carrot, onion, bell pepper, salt and black pepper in medium saucepan; cover with water. Bring to a boil. Cook 5 minutes or until tender; drain.

2. Combine soup and sour cream in 13×9-inch casserole; mix well. Stir in vegetable mixture and spread evenly. Sprinkle cheeses on top.

3. Top with dry stuffing mix. Bake, covered, 30 minutes or until heated through.

Makes 6 servings

summer squash casserole

carrie's sweet potato casserole

Carrie Anderson, Hyattsville, MD

    Topping (recipe follows)
 3 pounds sweet potatoes, cooked and peeled
 ½ cup (1 stick) butter, softened
 ½ cup sugar
 2 eggs, beaten
 ½ cup evaporated milk
 1 teaspoon vanilla
 1 cup chopped pecans

1. Prepare Topping; set aside. Preheat oven to 350°F. Grease 13×9-inch baking dish.

2. Mash sweet potatoes with butter in large bowl. Beat with electric mixer until light and fluffy.

3. One at a time, add sugar, eggs, evaporated milk and vanilla, beating after each addition. Spread in prepared baking dish. Spoon Topping over potatoes and sprinkle with pecans.

4. Bake 25 minutes or until set. Serve hot.   *Makes 8 to 12 servings*

Topping: Combine 1 cup packed light brown sugar, ½ cup all-purpose flour and ⅓ cup melted butter in medium bowl.

Hint: This casserole works well and looks pretty in individual serving dishes. Grease eight 6-ounce ovenproof ramekins and fill almost to the top with sweet potato mixture. Top as in the recipe above and bake 20 minutes at 350°F or until set.

carrie's sweet potato casserole

baked risotto with asparagus, spinach & parmesan

June Holmes, Alpharetta, GA

1 tablespoon olive oil
1 cup finely chopped onion
1 cup arborio (risotto) rice
8 cups (8 to 10 ounces) spinach leaves, torn into pieces
2 cups chicken broth
¼ teaspoon salt
¼ teaspoon ground nutmeg
½ cup grated Parmesan cheese, divided
1½ cups diagonally sliced asparagus

1. Preheat oven to 400°F. Spray 13×9-inch baking dish with nonstick cooking spray.

2. Heat olive oil in large skillet over medium-high heat. Add onion; cook and stir 4 minutes or until tender. Add rice and stir well.

3. Stir in spinach, a handful at a time adding more as it wilts. Add broth, salt and nutmeg. Reduce heat and simmer 7 minutes. Stir in ¼ cup cheese.

4. Transfer to prepared baking dish. Cover tightly and bake 15 minutes.

5. Remove from oven and stir in asparagus; sprinkle with remaining ¼ cup cheese. Cover and bake 15 minutes more or until liquid is absorbed. *Makes 6 servings*

baked risotto with asparagus, spinach & parmesan

polynesian baked beans

Lynda McCormick, Burkburnett, TX

2 tablespoons olive oil
3 tablespoons chopped onion
2 cans (16 ounces each) baked beans
1 can (about 11 ounces) mandarin oranges, drained
1 can (about 8 ounces) pineapple chunks in juice, drained
½ cup chopped green bell pepper
1 can (about 4 ounces) deviled ham
¼ cup ketchup
2 tablespoons packed brown sugar
½ teaspoon salt (optional)
  Dash hot pepper sauce

1. Preheat oven to 375°F. Heat oil in small skillet over medium heat. Add onion; cook and stir until transparent.

2. Combine onion and remaining ingredients in 2-quart casserole. Bake, uncovered, 30 to 35 minutes or until bubbly.

Makes 6 to 8 servings

Lynda says: This is a great recipe to double; it can also be made in a slow cooker.

crunchy top & flaky bottom broccoli casserole

Gloria Herdman, Pomeroy, OH

2 cans (8 ounces each) refrigerated crescent roll dough
1 package (16 ounces) frozen chopped broccoli
2 cups (8 ounces) shredded mozzarella cheese, divided
1½ cups French fried onions, coarsely crushed and divided
1 can (10¾ ounces) condensed cream of mushroom soup, undiluted
2 cans (5 ounces each) lean ham, drained and flaked
½ cup mayonnaise
2 eggs, beaten
2 tablespoons Dijon mustard
1 tablespoon prepared horseradish
1 jar (2 ounces) chopped pimientos, drained
1 teaspoon finely chopped parsley

1. Preheat oven to 375°F. Butter bottom of 13×9-inch baking dish. Unroll dough; do not separate. Press dough onto bottom of prepared baking dish, sealing all seams. Bake 7 minutes; remove from oven and set aside.

2. Combine broccoli, 1 cup cheese, ½ cup onions, soup, ham, mayonnaise, eggs, mustard and horseradish. Spread evenly over crust. Top with remaining 1 cup onions, 1 cup cheese, pimientos and parsley.

3. Bake for 20 to 25 minutes or until set. Cool 10 minutes before serving.   *Makes 8 servings*

mediterranean vegetable bake

Marilyn Pocius, Oak Park, IL

2 tomatoes, sliced
1 small red onion, sliced
1 medium zucchini, sliced
1 small eggplant, sliced
1 large portobello mushroom cap, sliced
2 cloves garlic, finely chopped
3 tablespoons olive oil
2 teaspoons chopped fresh rosemary
⅔ cup white wine
   Salt and black pepper

1. Preheat oven to 350°F. Oil bottom of 13×9-inch baking pan or 10-inch pie pan.

2. Arrange slices of vegetables in rows, alternating different types and overlapping slices in pan to make an attractive arrangement. Sprinkle garlic evenly over top. Mix olive oil with rosemary in small bowl; spread over top.

3. Pour wine over vegetables; season with salt and pepper. Loosely cover with foil. Bake 20 minutes. Uncover and bake an additional 10 to 15 minutes or until vegetables are soft.

Makes 4 to 6 servings

Marilyn says: Serve this with crusty bread to sop up the delicious juices. Feel free to use whatever vegetables you have on hand or in your garden.

mediterranean vegetable bake

bow tie zucchini

Karen Tellier, Cumberland, RI

¼ **cup vegetable oil**
1 **cup chopped onion**
2 **cloves garlic, minced**
5 **small zucchini, cut into thin strips**
⅔ **cup heavy cream**
1 **package (16 ounces) bow tie pasta, cooked and drained**
3 **tablespoons grated Parmesan cheese**
 Salt and black pepper

1. Preheat oven to 350°F.

2. Heat oil in large skillet over medium-high heat. Add onion and garlic; cook and stir until onion is tender. Add zucchini; cook and stir until tender.

3. Add cream; cook and stir until thickened. Add pasta and cheese to skillet. Season with salt and pepper to taste. Transfer mixture to 2-quart casserole. Cover and bake 15 minutes or until heated through.
Makes 8 servings

Helpful Hint: **Small and medium zucchini, up to 8 inches long, are more tender and have thinner skins than large zucchini.**

bow tie zucchini

spinach casserole

Charlotte G. Williams, St. Clair, PA

3 tablespoons butter
1 tablespoon all-purpose flour
1 cup milk
2 eggs, separated
1 tablespoon chopped fresh parsley
  Salt and black pepper
1 cup (4 ounces) shredded Cheddar cheese
2 packages (14 ounces each) frozen chopped spinach, thawed and squeezed dry

1. Preheat oven to 350°F. Butter 2½-quart casserole.

2. Melt butter in medium saucepan over medium heat. Stir in flour; cook and stir 2 minutes. Gradually whisk in milk. Continue cooking until mixture thickens slightly. Beat egg yolks. Gradually add egg yolks to milk mixture. Season with parsley, salt and pepper. Add cheese, stirring constantly until cheese melts. Transfer to medium bowl.

3. Add spinach to cheese sauce and stir until well combined; keep warm.

4. Beat egg whites in clean, dry bowl on high speed of electric mixer until stiff peaks form. Gently fold egg whites into spinach mixture.

5. Spoon into prepared casserole and bake 40 minutes or until center is set and looks dry. *Do not overbake.* *Makes 6 servings*

five-bean casserole

Susan Richardson, Portland, OR

2 medium onions, chopped
8 ounces bacon, diced
2 cloves garlic, minced
½ cup packed brown sugar
½ cup cider vinegar
1 teaspoon salt
1 teaspoon dry mustard
¼ teaspoon black pepper
2 cans (about 16 ounces each) kidney beans, rinsed and drained
1 can (about 16 ounces) chick-peas, rinsed and drained
1 can (about 16 ounces) butter beans, rinsed and drained
1 can (about 16 ounces) Great Northern or cannellini beans, rinsed and drained
1 can (about 16 ounces) baked beans

Slow Cooker Directions

1. Cook and stir onions, bacon and garlic in large skillet over medium heat until onions are tender; drain. Stir in brown sugar, vinegar, salt, mustard and pepper. Simmer over low heat 15 minutes.

2. Combine beans in slow cooker. Spoon onion mixture evenly over top. Cover; cook on HIGH 3 to 4 hours or on LOW 6 to 8 hours. *Makes 16 servings*

vegetable casserole

Adele Simoni, Whiting, NJ

1 package (about 16 ounces) frozen spinach
¾ cup (1½ sticks) unsalted butter, divided
   Salt and black pepper
8 potatoes, peeled and cooked until tender
1 cup milk
1 pound carrots, sliced and cooked until tender
1 pound green beans, cut into 1-inch pieces and cooked until tender
½ teaspoon paprika

1. Preheat oven to 375°F. Lightly grease 4-quart casserole or roasting pan.

2. Cook spinach according to package directions; drain and squeeze dry. Spread spinach in prepared casserole and dot with 1 tablespoon butter; season with salt and pepper.

3. Mash potatoes with milk and ½ cup butter until creamy.

4. Layer half of potatoes, carrots and beans over spinach. Dot with another 1 tablespoon butter; season with salt and pepper.

5. Layer with remaining half of potatoes. Dot with remaining 2 tablespoons butter and sprinkle with paprika. Bake 1 hour or until heated through and lightly browned.

Makes 10 to 12 servings

vegetable casserole

curried cauliflower & cashews

Marilyn Pocius, Oak Park, IL

1 medium head cauliflower, cut into florets (about 4 cups)
½ cup water
¾ cup toasted unsalted cashews
3 tablespoons butter, divided
2 tablespoons all-purpose flour
1 tablespoon curry powder
1¼ cups milk
Salt and black pepper
1 cup dry bread crumbs
Additional toasted unsalted cashews for garnish
1 jar prepared mango chutney (optional)

1. Preheat oven to 350°F. Butter 2-quart casserole.

2. Place cauliflower in large, microwavable dish. Add ½ cup water. Microwave at HIGH about 4 minutes or until almost tender. Drain and place in prepared casserole. Add ¾ cup cashews and stir until blended.

3. Melt 2 tablespoons butter in medium saucepan. Add flour and curry powder. Cook and stir over medium heat 2 minutes. Add milk, whisking constantly; cook and stir until mixture thickens slightly. Season with salt and pepper.

4. Pour sauce over cauliflower mixture and stir to coat evenly. Top with bread crumbs and dot with remaining 1 tablespoon butter.

5. Bake 45 minutes or until lightly browned. Garnish with additional cashews and serve with chutney, if desired.

Makes 8 servings

curried cauliflower & cashews

zucchini with feta casserole

June Holmes, Alpharetta, GA

4 medium zucchini, peeled
2 teaspoons butter or margarine
½ cup grated Parmesan cheese
2 eggs, beaten
⅓ cup crumbled feta cheese
2 tablespoons chopped fresh parsley
1 tablespoon all-purpose flour
2 teaspoons chopped fresh marjoram
  Dash hot pepper sauce
  Salt
  Black pepper

1. Preheat oven to 375°F. Grease 2-quart casserole.

2. Grate zucchini; drain in colander. Melt butter in medium skillet over medium heat. Add zucchini; cook and stir until slightly browned. Remove from heat.

3. Add remaining ingredients to skillet; mix well.

4. Pour into prepared casserole dish. Bake 35 minutes or until bubbly.   *Makes 4 servings*

wild rice casserole

Philip A. Pinchotti, Freedom, PA

    1 cup wild rice, soaked overnight
    1 large onion, chopped
    1 cup (4 ounces) shredded Cheddar cheese
    1 cup chopped mushrooms
    1 cup chopped black olives
    1 cup drained chopped canned tomatoes
    1 cup tomato juice
    ⅓ cup vegetable oil
    Salt and black pepper

1. Preheat oven to 350°F.

2. Drain rice. Combine rice and remaining ingredients except salt and pepper in large bowl.

3. Season with salt and pepper. Transfer rice mixture to 2½- to 3-quart casserole. Cover and bake 1½ hours or until rice is tender.   *Makes 6 servings*

Philip says: This tastes even better reheated the next day.

fruited corn pudding

Carole Resnick, Cleveland, OH

5 cups frozen corn, thawed and divided
5 eggs
½ cup milk
1½ cups heavy cream
⅓ cup unsalted butter, melted and cooled
1 teaspoon vanilla
½ teaspoon salt
¼ teaspoon ground nutmeg
3 tablespoons dried cranberries or raisins
3 tablespoons finely chopped dates
3 tablespoons finely chopped dried apricots
2 tablespoons finely chopped dried pears, or other dried fruit

1. Preheat oven to 350°F. Butter 13×9-inch baking dish; set aside.

2. In food processor, combine 3½ cups corn, eggs and milk; process until mixture is almost smooth.

3. Transfer corn mixture to large bowl. Add cream, butter, vanilla, salt and nutmeg; stir until well combined. Add remaining 1½ cups corn, cranberries, dates, apricots and pears. Stir well. Pour mixture into prepared baking dish.

4. Bake until pudding is set and top begins to brown, about 50 to 60 minutes. Remove from oven and allow to sit for 10 to 15 minutes before serving. *Makes 8 to 10 servings*

fruited corn pudding

my mac & cheese

Carrie A. Theroux, Saco, ME

4 tablespoons (½ stick) butter
4 tablespoons all-purpose flour
2 cups milk
½ pound sharp Cheddar cheese, cut into ½-inch cubes
8 slices (about 2 ounces) Pepper-Jack cheese, cut into pieces (optional)
½ cup chopped onion
2 cups (about 16 ounces) broccoli florets, steamed until tender
2 cups macaroni, cooked and drained
2 English muffins, cut into ½-inch pieces

1. Preheat oven to 350°F.

2. Melt butter in large saucepan over medium heat. Stir in flour; cook and stir 2 minutes. Gradually add milk, stirring contantly, until mixture is slightly thickened.

3. Add Cheddar cheese, Pepper-Jack cheese, if desired, and onion to the milk mixture. Cook, stirring constantly, until cheese melts.

4. Add broccoli; stir well.

5. Place macaroni in 3-quart casserole. Add cheese mixture; mix well. Sprinkle English muffin pieces evenly over top. Bake 15 to 20 minutes or until muffin pieces are golden brown.

Makes 4 to 6 servings

my mac & cheese

slow cooker veggie stew

Lin Tuschong, Fort Lauderdale, FL

    1 tablespoon vegetable oil
    ⅔ cup carrot slices
    ½ cup diced onion
    2 cloves garlic, chopped
    2 cans (14 ounces each) fat-free vegetable broth
 1½ cups chopped green cabbage
    ½ cup cut green beans
    ½ cup diced zucchini
    1 tablespoon tomato paste
    ½ teaspoon dried basil leaves
    ½ teaspoon dried oregano leaves
    ¼ teaspoon salt

Slow Cooker Directions

1. Heat oil in medium skillet over medium-high heat. Add carrot, onion and garlic. Cook and stir until tender.

2. Place carrot mixture and remaining ingredients in slow cooker; stir to combine. Cover; cook on LOW 8 to 10 hours or on HIGH 3 hours. *Makes 4 to 6 servings*

Helpful Hint: **When choosing fresh green beans for slow cooker recipes like this one, choose young, thin, crisp beans. Older beans may be tough.**

zucchini-carrot casserole

Sharon Morris, Neoga, IL

½ cup (1 stick) margarine, melted
1 package (about 6 ounces) herb-flavored stuffing mix
2 cups cubed fresh zucchini, blanched and drained
1 can (14 ounces) condensed cream of celery soup, undiluted
1 cup grated carrots
1 small onion, chopped
½ cup sour cream
½ cup (2 ounces) shredded Cheddar cheese

1. Preheat oven to 350°F.

2. Combine margarine and stuffing mix in medium bowl; set aside 1 cup for topping. Place remaining stuffing in 13×9-inch baking dish.

3. Combine zucchini, soup, carrots, onion and sour cream. Pour mixture over stuffing in baking dish. Top with remaining 1 cup stuffing mixture and cheese. Bake 40 to 45 minutes or until heated through and cheese is melted.   *Makes 8 servings*

BEST-LOVED PIES

mom's pumpkin pie

Penny Nichols, Baltimore, MD

1$^1/_2$ **cans (16 ounces each) solid pack pumpkin**
   1 **cup sugar**
   1 **can (12 ounces) evaporated milk**
   2 **eggs**
   2 **tablespoons maple syrup**
   1 **teaspoon ground cinnamon**
   1 **teaspoon vanilla**
  $^1/_2$ **teaspoon salt**
   2 **(9-inch) unbaked pie shells**
    Whipped cream (optional)

1. Preheat oven to 350°F. Combine all ingredients, except pie shells and whipped cream, in large bowl; mix well. Divide mixture evenly between pie shells.

2. Place pie pans on baking sheet. Bake 1 hour or until toothpick inserted in centers comes out clean. Cool. Top with whipped cream, if desired. *Makes 2 (9-inch) pies*

mom's pumpkin pie

fancy fudge pie

Tina M. Cartee, Mentor on the Lake, OH

    1 cup chocolate wafer crumbs
    ⅓ cup butter, melted
1⅓ cups (8 ounces) semisweet chocolate chips
    ½ cup (1 stick) butter, softened
    ¾ cup packed brown sugar
    3 eggs
    1 cup chopped pecans
    ½ cup all-purpose flour
    1 teaspoon vanilla
    ½ teaspoon instant espresso coffee powder
       Whipped cream or vanilla ice cream (optional)
       Chocolate syrup (optional)

1. Preheat oven to 375°F. Combine crumbs and melted butter in small bowl. Press onto bottom and up side of 9-inch pie pan. Bake 6 minutes. Remove from oven; cool.

2. Place chips in microwavable bowl. Microwave at HIGH 1 to 1½ minutes or just until chips are melted when stirred. Cool slightly. Beat softened butter and brown sugar in large bowl with electric mixer on medium speed until light and fluffy. Add eggs, one at a time, beating well after each addition. Stir in chocolate, pecans, flour, vanilla and espresso until blended.

3. Pour mixture into crust. Bake 30 to 40 minutes or until set. Cool completley; refrigerate. Serve chilled with whipped cream and chocolate syrup, if desired.   *Makes 8 servings*

brandy alexander pie

Leslee Crayne, Appleton, WI

    32 vanilla wafers
     3 cups vanilla ice cream, softened
     1 cup spiced egg nog
     1 cup frozen nondairy whipped topping, thawed
     1 package (4-serving size) vanilla-flavored instant pudding mix
     2 ounces brandy
     1 teaspoon vanilla
    ¼ teaspoon ground nutmeg
       Caramel ice cream topping (optional)

1. Line bottom and side of greased 9-inch pie pan with vanilla wafers.

2. Beat remaining ingredients, except caramel topping, in large bowl with electric mixer at low speed until well blended. *Do not overbeat.*

3. Pour mixture into prepared pie pan. Freeze until firm. Serve with caramel topping, if desired.

Makes 8 servings

Leslee says: For a nutty flavor, make this pie with butter pecan ice cream.

Helpful Hint: **To quickly soften ice cream, place it in a microwavable bowl and microwave at MEDIUM (50% power) for about 20 seconds or until slightly softened.**

raspberry cream pie

Linda Reiss, Sarasota, FL

½ **cup granulated sugar**
¼ **cup packed brown sugar**
3 **tablespoons all-purpose flour**
1 **tablespoon plus 1½ teaspoons ground cinnamon**
2 **cups whipping cream**
1 **teaspoon vanilla**
1 **package (12 ounces) frozen raspberries**
1 **(9-inch) unbaked deep-dish pie shell**

1. Preheat oven to 400°F. Combine sugars, flour and cinnamon in medium bowl. Add cream and vanilla; stir until smooth.

2. Separate raspberries and place in pie crust. Pour cream mixture over raspberries.

3. Bake 10 minutes. *Reduce oven temperature to 375°F.* Continue baking 55 to 65 minutes or until firm in center. Cool completely; refrigerate. *Makes 8 servings*

Linda says: Frozen blueberries or cherries can be substituted for the frozen raspberries.

raspberry cream pie

baked alaska apple butter pie

Eleanor Froehlich, Rochester Hills, MI

Pie pastry for single 9-inch pie crust
2 cups apple butter
1 can (13 ounces) evaporated milk
3 egg yolks, lightly beaten
¼ cup packed brown sugar
1 pint butter pecan ice cream
Brown Sugar Meringue (page 217)

1. Preheat oven to 425°F. Line 9-inch pie plate with pastry; crimp edge as desired.

2. Combine apple butter, evaporated milk, egg yolks and brown sugar in medium bowl; mix until well blended. Pour into pie crust. Bake 15 minutes. *Reduce oven temperature to 350°F.* Bake 45 minutes more or until thin knife inserted in center comes out clean. Cool pie on wire rack. Cover; refrigerate at least 1 hour or until ready to serve.

3. Meanwhile, allow ice cream to soften slightly. Cover inside of 8-inch pie plate with plastic wrap. Place ice cream in pie plate and spread evenly. Cover and place in freezer until firm.

4. Just before serving, preheat oven to 500°F. Prepare Brown Sugar Meringue. Using plastic wrap, unmold ice cream and invert onto prepared, chilled pie. Remove plastic wrap. Cover ice cream and any exposed surface of pie with meringue. Bake 2 to 3 minutes or until meringue is golden brown. Serve immediately

Makes 8 servings

brown sugar meringue

 3 egg whites
 ¼ teaspoon cream of tartar
 ½ teaspoon vanilla
 6 tablespoons brown sugar

Beat egg whites and cream of tartar in small bowl with electric mixer on high speed until foamy. Beat in vanilla. Add brown sugar, 1 tablespoon at a time; beat until stiff peaks form.

big al's coconut white-chocolate pie

Alan Wysong, Barlow, KY

 2½ cups milk
 1 package (4-serving size) white chocolate-flavored instant pudding mix
 1 package (4-serving size) coconut cream-flavored instant pudding mix
 1 (9-inch) prepared graham cracker crust
 1 container (8 ounces) frozen whipped topping, thawed

1. Combine milk and pudding mixes in large bowl. Beat with whisk until smooth and thick. Pour into crust.

2. Refrigerate at least 1 hour.

3. Serve with whipped topping.   *Makes 8 to 12 servings*

rustic apple tart with crème chantilly

Rebecca Hunt, Santa Paula, CA

Rustic Tart Dough (page 220)
2 pounds Golden Delicious apples, peeled, cored and cut into ½-inch wedges
2 tablespoons freshly squeezed lemon juice
½ cup plus 2 tablespoons sugar, divided
½ cup raisins
3 tablespoons plus 1½ teaspoons Calvados,* divided
1 teaspoon ground cinnamon
3 tablespoons unsalted butter, cut into 6 to 8 pieces
1 cup apricot jam
Crème Chantilly (page 220)

Calvados is an apple brandy. Any brandy or cognac can be substituted.

1. Prepare Rustic Tart Dough.

2. Preheat oven to 400°F. Toss apples with lemon juice in large bowl. Add ½ cup sugar, raisins, 2 tablespoons Calvados and cinnamon. Toss gently to mix; set aside.

3. Cut piece of parchment paper to fit 15×2-inch baking sheet or jelly-roll pan. Place parchment on flat work surface and lightly flour. Place dough on parchment. Lightly flour top of dough. Roll out into 18×16-inch oval about ¼ inch thick. Transfer parchment and dough to baking sheet.

4. Place apple mixture onto center of dough, spreading to within 2 inches of edge. Dot filling with butter. Fold edge of dough over filling, overlapping as necessary. Press gently to seal (the center of the tart will remain open). Sprinkle edge of dough with remaining 2 tablespoons sugar.

5. Bake 50 to 55 minutes or until tart dough is browned and apples are tender. Cool slightly.

continued on page 220

rustic apple tart with crème chantilly

rustic apple tart with crème chantilly, continued

6. Strain jam through sieve into small saucepan. Cook over low heat until jam is smooth. Stir in remaining Calvados; keep warm. Brush warm tart with jam mixture. Serve with Crème Chantilly.

Makes 8 servings

rustic tart dough

- **2 cups all-purpose flour**
- **1 teaspoon sugar**
- **1 teaspoon grated lemon peel**
- **½ teaspoon salt**
- **½ teaspoon ground cinnamon**
- **½ cup vegetable shortening, chilled**
- **½ cup (1 stick) unsalted cold butter, cut into ¼-inch dice**
- **⅓ cup ice water**

1. Place flour, sugar, lemon peel, salt and cinnamon in food processor; process briefly.

2. Add shortening; process using on/off pulsing action until shortening is pea size. Add butter; process using on/off pulsing action until dough resembles coarse crumbs. Add ice water; process just until dough begins to come together. Shape dough into 6-inch disc; wrap in plastic wrap. Refrigerate at least 1 hour or overnight.

crème chantilly

- **1 cup whipping cream**
- **1 tablespoon Calvados**
- **½ to 1 tablespoon sugar**

Whip cream in chilled medium bowl with chilled beaters just until soft peaks form. Add Calvados and sugar to taste, beating until definite peaks form. *Do not overbeat*. Refrigerate until ready to serve.

citrus custard pie

Merrilee Powers, Troy, MI

½ **cup sugar**
½ **cup orange juice**
1 **package (4-serving size) vanilla-flavored instant pudding mix**
3 **tablespoons butter**
2 **tablespoons lemon juice**
3 **eggs**
1 **cup orange marmalade**
1 **teaspoon vanilla**
1 **(9-inch) graham cracker crust**
2 **cups peeled orange sections**

1. Combine sugar, orange juice, pudding mix, butter and lemon juice in top of 2-quart double boiler over simmering water. Whisk until well blended. Beat eggs lightly in small bowl. Whisk into pudding mixture. Cook and stir until mixture thickens (160°F). *Do not boil*. Remove from heat; stir in marmalade and vanilla.

2. Pour into prepared crust. Let cool. Refrigerate until firm. Serve chilled with orange sections.

Makes 8 servings

Tip: Using a double boiler to cook an egg mixture will help to prevent curdling. The bottom pan should contain hot, not boiling, water. Be sure there is space between the water and the top pan.

favorite peanut butter pie

Carolyn Blakemore, Fairmont, WV

¾ cup creamy peanut butter, divided
1 prepared (9-inch) shortbread pie crust
½ cup peanut butter chips, divided
1 package (3 ounces) cream cheese, softened
1 cup powdered sugar
1 container (8 ounces) frozen nondairy whipped topping, thawed

1. Spread ¼ cup peanut butter over bottom of pie crust. Sprinkle with ¼ cup peanut butter chips.

2. Beat cream cheese and sugar in medium bowl with electric mixer; beat in remaining ½ cup peanut butter until light and fluffy. Fold in whipped topping.

3. Pour into pie crust and sprinkle with remaining peanut butter chips. Serve immediately or refrigerate. *Makes 8 servings*

favorite peanut butter pie

spiced raisin custard pie

Lorinda Platti, Germantown, NY

1½ cups raisins
1 teaspoon sugar
3 teaspoons ground cinnamon, divided
1 can (14 ounces) sweetened condensed milk
1 cup biscuit and baking mix (or reduced-fat biscuit and baking mix)
1 cup applesauce
½ cup sugar
3 eggs
¼ cup (½ stick) butter or margarine, melted
2 teaspoons vanilla
1 teaspoon ground nutmeg
1 container (8 ounces) frozen nondairy whipped topping, thawed

1. Preheat oven to 325°F. Spray 10-inch glass pie plate with nonstick cooking spray. Set aside.

2. Place raisins in small bowl, separating any that may be stuck together. Combine sugar and 1 teaspoon cinnamon in small bowl; mix well. Reserve 1 teaspoon sugar mixture. Sprinkle remaining sugar mixture over raisins. Toss to coat.

3. Combine all remaining ingredients, except whipped topping, in large bowl. Beat 2 minutes with electric mixer on medium speed or until well blended. Pour into prepared pie plate. Bake 10 minutes.

4. Remove from oven; top with raisin mixture and sprinkle with reserved sugar mixture. Bake 35 to 40 minutes more (center will be soft). Cool to room temperature; refrigerate at least 2 hours. Serve chilled with whipped topping. Refrigerate leftover pie. *Makes 12 servings*

lemon meringue pie

Catherine Gooch, Colorado Springs, CO

1 baked (9-inch) deep-dish pie crust
1 package (11 ounces) vanilla wafers
1 can (14 ounces) sweetened condensed milk
½ cup lemon juice
2 eggs, separated
3 tablespoons marshmallow creme
   Pinch of salt

1. Cover bottom of pie crust with vanilla wafers, reserving some for garnish.

2. Beat condensed milk, lemon juice and egg yolks in top of 2-quart double boiler set over simmering water with electric mixer at low speed. Cook, beating constantly, until mixture thickens and reaches 160°F. *Do not boil*. Remove from heat.

3. Pour egg mixture over vanilla wafers in pie crust; decorate edge with reserved vanilla wafers. Cool to room temperature; refrigerate until ready to serve.

4. Preheat oven to 350°F. Just before serving, beat egg whites and marshmallow creme in medium bowl with electric mixer until stiff peaks form. Spoon onto pie, pulling up decorative peaks with tip of spoon. Bake until meringue is golden brown. *Makes 8 servings*

Helpful Hint: **Spread meringue over the filling and seal it to the edge of the crust. This will help to prevent the meringue from shrinking away from the crust when it is baked.**

italian chocolate pie alla lucia

Bessie Turner, Royal Oak, MI

¹/₄ cup pine nuts
3 tablespoons packed brown sugar
1 tablespoon grated orange peel
1 (9-inch) unbaked pie shell
4 ounces bittersweet chocolate, coarsely chopped
3 tablespoons unsalted butter
1 can (5 ounces) evaporated milk
3 eggs
3 tablespoons hazelnut liqueur
1 teaspoon vanilla
   Whipped cream (optional)
   Chocolate curls (optional)

1. Toast pine nuts in dry nonstick skillet over medium heat, stirring constantly until golden brown and aromatic. Remove from heat and finely chop; cool. Combine pine nuts, brown sugar and orange peel in small bowl. Sprinkle onto bottom of prepared pie shell and gently press into place with fingertips or back of spoon.

2. Preheat oven to 325°F. Melt chocolate and butter in small saucepan over low heat. Stir well to blend. Let cool to room temperature.

3. Beat chocolate mixture with evaporated milk in medium bowl with electric mixer at medium speed. Add eggs, one at a time, beating well after each addition. Stir in hazelnut liqueur and vanilla. Pour into pie shell over pine nut mixture.

4. Bake on center rack of oven 30 to 40 minutes or until filling is set.

5. Cool completely on wire rack. Refrigerate until ready to serve. Serve with whipped cream and chocolate curls, if desired.

Makes 8 servings

Bessie says: This pie is beautiful when garnished with chocolate curls. To make chocolate curls, melt ½ cup semisweet chocolate chips and 1 teaspoon vegetable oil in medium microwavable bowl at MEDIUM (50% power) 1 minute. Stir well. Spread chocolate mixture in 2-inch-wide ribbons on parchment paper. Let set for 1 minute, then using the edge of a spatula, scrape chocolate into curls. Place the curls on parchment paper to set.

speedy strawberry pie

Ellis Rice, Hillsboro, OR

⅓ cup butter
1 cup vanilla wafer crumbs
3 containers (4 ounces each) strawberry yogurt
1 package (4-serving size) vanilla-flavored instant pudding mix
2 tablespoons butter, softened
1 package (8 ounces) cream cheese, softened
1 cup strawberry preserves
1 teaspoon vanilla
1 cup fresh sliced strawberries

1. Preheat oven to 350°F. Melt ⅓ cup butter in small saucepan. Combine butter and crumbs in small bowl. Press onto bottom and up side of 9-inch pie plate. Bake 8 minutes. Cool.

2. Beat yogurt, pudding mix and 2 tablespoons softened butter in medium bowl with electric mixer at medium speed until smooth. Beat in cream cheese, strawberry preserves and vanilla until well blended.

3. Pour into pie shell. Refrigerate until firm. Serve chilled with fresh sliced strawberries.

Makes 8 servings

apple crunch pie

Jacki Remsberg, Carson City, NV

     1 refrigerated pie crust (½ of 15-ounce package)
1¼ cups all-purpose flour, divided
     1 cup granulated sugar
     6 tablespoons melted butter, divided
1½ teaspoons ground cinnamon, divided
     ¾ teaspoon ground nutmeg, divided
     ½ teaspoon ground ginger
     ¼ teaspoon salt
     4 cups peeled, cored, diced apples
     ½ cup packed brown sugar
     ½ cup chopped walnuts

1. Preheat oven to 350°F. Place crust in 9-inch pie pan; flute edge as desired.

2. Combine ¼ cup flour, granulated sugar, 2 tablespoons butter, 1 teaspoon cinnamon, ½ teaspoon nutmeg, ginger and salt. Mix well. Add apples and toss to coat. Place apple mixture into pie crust.

3. Combine remaining 1 cup flour, brown sugar, walnuts, remaining 4 tablespoons butter, ½ teaspoon cinnamon and ¼ teaspoon nutmeg; sprinkle evenly on top of apple mixture.

4. Bake 45 to 55 minutes or until apples are tender.   *Makes 8 servings*

apple crunch pie

pineapple cream cheese pie

Myria Estes, Cullman, AL

1 package (8 ounces) cream cheese, softened
1 can (20 ounces) crushed pineapple, drained and juice reserved
2 cups cold milk
2 packages (4-serving size) vanilla-flavored instant pudding mix
2 (9-inch) graham cracker crusts
   Whipped topping

1. Beat cream cheese, reserved pineapple juice and milk 1 minute in medium bowl with electric mixer on high speed until smooth. Add pudding mix; beat until smooth. Stir in pineapple.

2. Pour into crusts; refrigerate until set. Serve with whipped topping.   *Makes 16 servings*

Myria says: For reduced-sugar pies, use pineapple in its own juice and substitute sugar-free instant pudding mix.

Helpful Hint: To soften cream cheese quickly, remove it from its wrapper and place it in a medium microwavable bowl. Microwave it at MEDIUM (50% power) for 15 to 20 seconds or until the cream cheese is slightly softened.

chocolate root beer rocky road pie

Connie Emerson, Reno, NV

1½ cups crushed chocolate wafers, plus additional for garnish
¼ to ½ cup powdered sugar
6 tablespoons butter, melted
1 can (14 ounces) sweetened condensed milk
3 egg yolks, beaten
1 tablespoon root beer extract
1 cup miniature marshmallows
¾ cup chopped pecans
Whipped cream, for garnish (optional)

1. Preheat oven to 325°F.

2. Combine wafer crumbs, powdered sugar and butter in large bowl; mix well. Press firmly into 9-inch pie plate.

3. Beat milk, egg yolks and extract in large bowl with electric mixer at medium speed 2 minutes. Stir in marshmallows and pecans. Pour mixture into crust. Bake 30 minutes or until knife inserted in center comes out clean. Cool completely on wire rack. Garnish with additional wafer crumbs and whipped cream, if desired. *Makes 6 to 8 servings*

kathy's key lime pie

Debbie Gerrie, Grants, NM

> 1 package (8 ounces) cream cheese, softened
> 1 package (4-serving size) lime-flavored gelatin mix
> 2 containers (8 ounces each) frozen nondairy whipped topping, thawed
> 1 (9-inch) graham cracker pie crust

1. Beat cream cheese, gelatin and ⅔ of whipped topping in large bowl with electric mixer on medium speed until smooth.

2. Spoon into pie crust; top with remaining whipped topping. Serve immediately or refrigerate until ready to serve.

Makes 8 servings

rhubarb tart

Marilyn Pocius, Oak Park, IL

> Pie pastry for single 9-inch pie crust
> 4 cups rhubarb, cut into ½-inch pieces
> 1¼ cups sugar
> ¼ cup all-purpose flour
> 2 tablespoons butter, cut into chunks
> ¼ cup uncooked old-fashioned oats

1. Preheat oven to 450°F. Line 9-inch pie plate with pastry; set aside.

2. Combine rhubarb, sugar and flour in medium bowl. Pour into pie crust. Top with butter. Sprinkle oats over rhubarb. Bake 10 minutes. *Reduce oven temperature to 350°F.* Bake 40 minutes more or until bubbly.

Makes 8 servings

kathy's key lime pie

canadian butter tarts

Lillian Porter, Deltona, IL

¼ **cup (½ stick) butter**
½ **cup packed brown sugar**
½ **cup dark corn syrup**
 1 **egg**
½ **cup chopped walnuts**
¼ **cup golden raisins**
½ **teaspoon vanilla**
¼ **teaspoon salt**
 8 **unbaked medium tart shells**

1. Preheat oven to 375°F. Beat butter in medium bowl with electric mixer at medium speed until creamy. Gradually beat in sugar and corn syrup.

2. Add egg and beat until light; stir in walnuts, raisins, vanilla and salt.

3. Spoon into unbaked tart shells. Bake 8 minutes.

4. *Reduce oven temperature to 350°F.* Bake 12 to 13 minutes more or until filling is set and tart shells are lightly browned.

Makes 8 servings

hawaiian paradise pie

Patricia Harmon, Baden, PA

    Pie pastry for single 9-inch pie crust
2 eggs
½ cup coarsely chopped pecans
½ cup coarsely chopped macadamia nuts
⅓ cup corn syrup (half light corn syrup, half dark corn syrup)
1 can (21 ounces) pineapple pie filling
½ teaspoon ground cinnamon
1 package (8 ounces) cream cheese, softened
⅓ cup sugar
1 teaspoon vanilla
Whipped topping

1. Preheat oven to 375°F. Place pastry in pie plate; flute edge as desired.

2. Beat 1 egg in medium bowl, then stir in nuts and corn syrup. Pour into pie crust. Bake 15 to 20 minutes or until partially set.

3. Meanwhile, combine pineapple pie filling and cinnamon in medium bowl; set aside. Beat cream cheese and sugar in medium bowl with electric mixer on medium speed until fluffy. Add remaining 1 egg and vanilla; beat until smooth.

4. Remove pie from oven; carefully spoon pineapple mixture on top. Spoon cream cheese mixture on top of pineapple mixture, spreading evenly to crust.

5. Bake 20 to 25 minutes or until filling is set. If necessary, cover crust with foil during last 10 minutes to prevent overbrowning. Remove from oven and cool to room temperature. Refrigerate until chilled. Serve with whipped topping. *Makes 8 to 10 servings*

apple-pear praline pie

Stacy Dent, Honolulu, HI

6 cups peeled, cored, thinly sliced Granny Smith (or other variety) apples
3 cups peeled, cored, thinly sliced pears
¾ cup granulated sugar
¼ cup plus 1 tablespoon all-purpose flour, divided
4 tablespoons ground cinnamon
¼ teaspoon salt
1 package (15 ounces) refrigerated pie crusts (2 crusts)
2 tablespoons butter, cut into pieces
½ cup (1 stick) butter
1 cup packed brown sugar
¼ cup half-and-half
1 cup chopped pecans

1. Preheat oven to 350°F.

2. Combine apples, pears, granulated sugar, ¼ cup flour, cinnamon and salt in large bowl; toss gently to mix. Set aside. Line 9-inch deep-dish pie pan with pie crust; dust lightly with remaining 1 tablespoon flour. Spoon apple and pear mixture into pie crust. Dot with 2 tablespoons butter. Top with second pie crust and flute as desired; cut slits in crust to vent steam.

3. Bake 50 to 55 minutes. Remove pie from oven.

4. Melt remaining ½ cup butter in small saucepan over low heat. Stir in brown sugar and half-and-half. Bring mixture to a boil on medium-high heat, stirring constantly. Remove from heat; stir in pecans. Spread over top of pie.

5. Place pie on baking sheet; bake 5 minutes. Remove from oven. Cool 1 hour or more before serving.

Makes 8 servings

apple-pear praline pie

pumpkin pecan pie

Beth Spam, Glasgow, KY

  1 can (15 ounces) solid pack pumpkin
  1 can (14 ounces) condensed milk
  ¼ cup butter, softened
  2 eggs
  1 teaspoon ground cinnamon
  1 teaspoon vanilla
  ½ teaspoon ground nutmeg
  ¼ teaspoon salt
  1 (9-inch) graham cracker pie crust
  2 tablespoons packed brown sugar
  2 tablespoons dark corn syrup
  1 tablespoon melted butter
  ½ teaspoon maple flavoring
  1 cup chopped pecans

1. Preheat oven to 400°F.

2. Combine pie filling, condensed milk, softened butter, 1 egg, cinnamon, vanilla, nutmeg and salt in large bowl. Pour into pie crust. Bake 20 minutes.

3. Beat remaining egg, brown sugar, corn syrup, melted butter and maple flavoring in medium bowl with electric mixer on medium speed. Stir in pecans.

4. Remove pie from oven; top with pecan mixture. *Reduce oven temperature to 350°F.* Bake 25 minutes more or until knife inserted in center comes out clean.   *Makes 8 to 10 servings*

mother's coconut pie

Mary G. Taylor, Murfreesboro, TN

1¼ cups sugar, divided
½ cup self-rising flour
1¼ cups milk
3 eggs, separated
1 teaspoon vanilla
2 tablespoons butter or margarine
1¼ cups shredded coconut, divided
1 baked (9-inch) pie crust

1. Preheat oven to 350°F.

2. Combine 1 cup sugar and flour in 2-quart saucepan. Whisk in milk, egg yolks, vanilla and butter until well blended. Cook, stirring constantly, over medium heat until mixture thickens. Remove from heat; add 1 cup coconut. Spoon into crust.

3. Beat egg whites in medium bowl with electric mixer on high speed until foamy. Slowly add remaining ¼ cup sugar; beat until stiff peaks form. Spoon on top of pie. Sprinkle remaining ¼ cup coconut on top; bake 10 to 15 minutes or until egg white mixture is golden brown. Remove from oven. Cool. Refrigerate leftover pie. *Makes 8 servings*

buttermilk pie

Edna Ash, Nashville, TN

1½ cups sugar
 1 tablespoon cornstarch
 3 eggs
 ½ cup buttermilk
 ½ cup butter, melted
 1 tablespoon lemon juice
 1 teaspoon vanilla
 1 (9-inch) graham cracker pie crust
    Whipped cream (optional)

1. Preheat oven to 350°F.

2. Combine sugar and cornstarch in medium bowl. Whisk in eggs, buttermilk, butter, lemon juice and vanilla. Beat with electric mixer on medium speed until smooth.

3. Pour into pie crust.

4. Bake 40 to 50 minutes or until set. Cool to room temperature; refrigerate. Serve chilled with whipped cream, if desired.

Makes 8 servings

Helpful Hint: To release more juice from lemons, warm them to room temperature. Then, roll around on the counter under the flat of your hand to release juice from the small sacs of the lemon.

creamy vanilla apple pie

Heather Williams, Paola, KS

1 egg
6 to 8 apples, peeled, cored and sliced ¼ inch thick
1 cup sugar
1 cup vanilla-flavored yogurt
4 to 6 tablespoons all-purpose flour
1 teaspoon vanilla
½ teaspoon ground cinnamon
1 unbaked 9-inch pie crust
    Spicy Crumb Topping (recipe follows)

1. Preheat oven to 350°F. Beat egg in medium bowl; add apples, sugar, yogurt, flour, vanilla and cinnamon. Stir to coat apples; pour into pie crust.

2. Prepare Spicy Crumb Topping. Sprinkle over apple mixture.

3. Bake 1 hour or until topping is golden brown   *Makes 8 servings*

spicy crumb topping

1 cup all-purpose flour
½ cup granulated sugar
½ cup packed brown sugar
½ cup (1 stick) butter, melted
¼ teaspoon ground cinnamon

Combine all ingredients in medium bowl; stir to combine.

TREASURED CAKES

jo's moist and delicious chocolate cake

Jo Skinner, Miami, FL

  2 cups all-purpose flour
  1 cup sugar
  4 tablespoons cocoa
  1½ teaspoons baking powder
  1½ teaspoons baking soda
  1 cup mayonnaise
  1 cup hot coffee
  2 teaspoons vanilla

1. Preheat oven to 350°F. Grease and flour 10-inch Bundt pan. Set aside.

2. Sift together flour, sugar, cocoa, baking powder and baking soda. Stir in mayonnaise, coffee and vanilla until batter is smooth. Pour into prepared pan.

3. Bake 30 minutes or until toothpick inserted near center comes out clean. Cool 10 to 15 minutes on wire rack; remove from pan to wire rack. Cool completely.   *Makes 12 servings*

Jo says: Frost this cake with your favorite icing or glaze. It's also delicious sprinkled with powdered sugar!

jo's moist and delicious chocolate cake

angel food cake roll

Tammy J. Christiansen, Dixon, IL

> 1 package (16 ounces) angel food cake mix, plus ingredients to prepare cake
> ¼ cup plus 2 tablespoons powdered sugar, divided
> 1 cup cold milk
> 1 package (4-serving size) vanilla-flavored instant pudding mix
> 1 cup whipping cream

1. Preheat oven 350°F.

2. Line bottom of 15×10-inch jelly-roll pan with waxed paper. Prepare cake mix according to package directions; pour batter into prepared pan. Bake 20 minutes or until cake is golden brown and springs back when lightly touched. Cool 15 minutes. Lay clean towel on flat surface. Sift ¼ cup powdered sugar over towel. Invert cake onto towel. Carefully peel off waxed paper. Starting at short end of cake, roll up with towel, jelly-roll style. Cool 30 minutes, seam side down, on wire rack.

3. Beat milk and pudding mix 2 minutes in large bowl with electric mixer at low speed. Let stand 5 minutes. Beat whipping cream in separate bowl with electric mixer at high speed until soft peaks form. Fold whipped cream into pudding mixture.

4. Unroll cake. Spread filling to within 1 inch of edges of cake. Reroll and place, seam side down, on serving plate. Dust with remaining 2 tablespoons powdered sugar. *Makes 8 servings*

blueberry crumb cake

Constance McMorris, Newberry, SC

2 cups all-purpose flour
⅔ cup sugar
1 tablespoon baking powder
1 teaspoon salt
½ teaspoon baking soda
1 cup milk
½ cup (1 stick) butter or margarine, melted
2 eggs, beaten
2 tablespoons lemon juice
2 cups frozen or fresh blueberries
Crumb Topping (recipe follows)

1. Preheat oven to 375°F. Grease 13×9-inch baking pan. Set aside.

2. Sift flour, sugar, baking powder, salt and baking soda into large bowl.

3. Combine milk, butter, eggs and lemon juice in medium bowl. Pour into flour mixture. Stir until blended.

4. Pour into prepared pan. Sprinkle blueberries evenly over batter. Prepare Crumb Topping.

5. Sprinkle cake with Crumb Topping; bake 40 to 45 minutes. Serve warm.

Makes 6 to 8 servings

Crumb Topping: Combine 1 cup chopped walnuts or pecans, ⅔ cup sugar, ½ cup all-purpose flour, 4 tablespoons softened butter or margarine and ½ teaspoon cinnamon in large bowl until mixture forms coarse crumbs.

white chocolate pecan caramel cheesecake

Josephine Devereaux Piro, Easton, PA

   7 whole graham crackers
   ¼ cup butter, cut into pieces
   1 cup reduced-fat sour cream
   4 eggs, separated
   ½ cup sugar
   1 tablespoon cornstarch
   3 packages (8 ounces each) ⅓-less-fat cream cheese, softened
   5 squares (1 ounce each) white baking chocolate, melted and cooled slightly
   2 tablespoons fresh lemon juice
   2 teaspoons vanilla
   2 tablespoons hot fudge ice cream topping
   2 tablespoons caramel ice cream topping
   ½ cup coarsely chopped pecans
   ⅓ cup semisweet mini chocolate chips

1. Preheat oven to 325°F. Grease 9-inch springform pan with nonstick cooking spray. Set aside.

2. Break graham crackers into food processor or blender; process using on/off pulsing action until finely crushed. Add butter; process using on/off pulsing action until mixture resembles fine crumbs. Press crumb mixture into bottom and up side of prepared pan. Set aside.

3. Beat sour cream, egg yolks, sugar and cornstarch in large bowl with electric mixer at medium speed until smooth. Add cream cheese, white chocolate, lemon juice and vanilla; beat until well blended.

4. Beat egg whites in large bowl until stiff peaks form. Fold egg white mixture into cream cheese mixture. Pour into prepared crust. Bake 15 minutes or until center jiggles slightly when shaken. Turn off oven and let cake cool 1 hour. Cool in pan on wire rack 10 minutes. Carefully run thin knife around edge of pan to release cake. Cool completely.

continued on page 248

white chocolate pecan caramel cheesecake

white chocolate pecan caramel cheesecake, continued

5. Remove side of pan; place cheesecake on serving plate. Drizzle with hot fudge and caramel ice cream toppings. Sprinkle with pecans and chips. Cover; refrigerate 4 hours or overnight. Remove from refrigerator 1 hour before serving. *Makes 12 to 16 servings*

applesauce cake

Jamie H. Mozingo, La Pine, OR

    2 cups sugar
 1½ cups applesauce
  ½ cup shortening
  ½ cup water
    2 eggs, beaten
 2¾ cups all-purpose flour
 1½ teaspoons baking soda
  ¾ teaspoon ground cinnamon
  ½ teaspoon ground cloves
  ½ teaspoon ground allspice
  ¼ teaspoon baking powder
    1 cup raisins
  ½ cup chopped walnuts

1. Preheat oven to 350°F. Grease 13×9-inch baking dish; set aside.

2. Combine sugar, applesauce, shortening, water and eggs in large bowl until blended.

3. Combine flour, baking soda, cinnamon, cloves, allspice and baking powder in medium bowl. Gradually stir flour mixture into applesauce mixture. Stir in raisins and walnuts.

4. Pour batter into prepared pan. Bake 25 to 30 minutes or until toothpick inserted into center comes out clean. *Makes 12 to 15 servings*

butter brickle cake

Marci Carl, Northern Cambria, PA

⅔ cup sugar
2 teaspoons ground cinnamon
1 package (about 18 ounces) yellow cake mix
1 package (4-serving size) butterscotch-flavored instant pudding mix
4 eggs
¾ cup oil
¾ cup water
1 cup chopped walnuts, divided

1. Preheat oven to 350°F. Grease and flour 13×9-inch cake pan. Combine sugar and cinnamon in small bowl; set aside.

2. Combine cake mix, pudding mix, eggs, oil and water in large bowl. Beat 4 to 5 minutes with electric mixer on medium speed or until batter is fluffy. Pour half of cake batter into prepared pan. Sprinkle ½ cup walnuts evenly on top. Sprinkle with half of cinnamon-sugar mixture. Cover with remaining cake batter. Sprinkle remaining walnuts onto batter. Sprinkle with remaining cinnamon-sugar mixture.

3. Bake 40 to 45 minutes or until toothpick inserted into center comes out clean. Cool completely in pan on wire rack.

Makes 12 to 15 servings

Marci says: This cake is great served warm from the oven, topped with whipped cream or partially melted vanilla ice cream!

orange kiss me cake

Rebecca Norman, Fremont, OH

    1 large orange
    1 cup raisins
 ⅔ cup chopped walnuts, divided
    2 cups all-purpose flour
1⅓ cups sugar, divided
    1 teaspoon baking soda
    1 teaspoon salt
    1 cup milk, divided
 ½ cup shortening
    2 eggs
    1 teaspoon ground cinnamon

1. Preheat oven to 350°F. Grease and flour 6 (4-inch) miniature Bundt pans or 1 (10-inch) Bundt pan.

2. Juice orange. Reserve ⅓ cup juice. Coarsely chop remaining orange pulp and peel. Process pulp, peel, raisins and ⅓ cup walnuts in food processor fitted with metal blade until ground.

3. Sift flour, 1 cup sugar, baking soda and salt together in large bowl. Add ¾ cup milk and shortening. Beat 2 minutes with electric mixer at medium speed until well blended. Beat 2 minutes more. Add eggs and remaining ¼ cup milk; beat 2 minutes. Fold orange mixture into batter; mix well. Pour into prepared pans.

4. Bake 40 to 45 minutes or until toothpick inserted near center comes out clean. Cool in pan 15 minutes. Invert onto serving plate. Poke holes in cake with wooden skewer or fork tines.

5. Pour reserved juice over cake. Combine remaining ⅓ cup sugar, ⅓ cup walnuts and cinnamon in small bowl. Sprinkle over cake. Garnish as desired.

Makes 12 servings

orange kiss me cakes

frozen chocolate cookie cake

Gina Cramer, Noah Branch, MI

30 chocolate creme-filled sandwich cookies
¾ cup (1½ sticks) butter, divided
½ gallon vanilla ice cream, softened
1 can (16 ounces) chocolate syrup
1 can (14 ounces) sweetened condensed milk
1 container (8 ounces) frozen whipped topping, thawed
    Chopped nuts (optional)

1. Finely crush cookies in resealable plastic food storage bag with rolling pin or in blender. Sprinkle onto bottom of 13×9-inch pan. Melt ¼ cup butter in small saucepan. Pour over cookies in pan. Freeze 15 minutes.

2. Spread ice cream over crust. Freeze 15 minutes.

3. Combine chocolate syrup, condensed milk and remaining ½ cup butter in medium saucepan. Bring to a boil; cook and stir 1 minute. Cool slightly.

4. Pour chocolate syrup mixture over ice cream. Spread whipped topping over chocolate syrup mixture. Sprinkle with nuts, if desired. Freeze until firm. *Makes 10 to 12 servings*

butterscotch bundt cake

Valery Anderson, Roseville, MI

1 package (18¼ ounces) yellow cake mix
1 package (4-serving size) butterscotch-flavored instant pudding mix
1 cup water
3 eggs
2 teaspoons ground cinnamon
½ cup chopped pecans
   Powdered sugar (optional)

1. Preheat oven to 325°F. Spray 10-inch Bundt pan with nonstick cooking spray.

2. Combine all ingredients, except pecans and powdered sugar, in large bowl. Beat 2 minutes with electric mixer at medium-high speed until blended. Stir in pecans. Pour into prepared pan.

3. Bake 40 to 50 minutes or until cake springs back when lightly touched. Cool on wire rack 10 minutes. Invert cake onto serving plate. Cool completely. Sprinkle with powdered sugar, if desired.   *Makes 12 to 16 servings*

Valery says: Try substituting white cake mix for yellow cake mix, pistachio pudding for butterscotch pudding and walnuts for pecans for a delicious Pistachio Bundt Cake with Walnuts.

peanut butter cup cheesecake

James Morrow, Riverbank, CA

2 cups chocolate wafer crumbs
⅓ cup margarine, melted
2 packages (8 ounces each) cream cheese, softened and divided
¾ cup plus 1 tablespoon sugar, divided
½ cup chunky-style peanut butter
1 tablespoon plus 1½ teaspoons all-purpose flour
3 eggs
¼ cup milk
2 squares (1 ounce each) semisweet chocolate, melted
⅛ teaspoon vanilla
Miniature peanut butter cups, cut in half, for garnish (optional)

1. Preheat oven to 325°F. Combine wafer crumbs and margarine in small bowl until blended; press onto bottom and up side of 9-inch springform pan. Bake 10 minutes.

2. Combine 1 package cream cheese, ½ cup sugar, peanut butter and flour in large bowl. Beat 2 minutes with electric mixer at medium speed or until well blended. (Batter will be very stiff.) Add 2 eggs, one at a time, beating well after each addition. Blend in milk. Pour cream cheese mixture evenly over crust.

3. *Increase oven temperature to 450°F.* Beat remaining 1 package cream cheese and ¼ cup plus 1 tablespoon remaining sugar 2 minutes in medium bowl with electric mixer at medium speed until well blended. Add egg; mix well. Blend in chocolate and vanilla; spoon over peanut butter layer. Spread chocolate layer carefully to seal.

4. Bake 10 minutes. *Reduce oven temperature to 250°F.* Bake 40 minutes or until set.

5. Cool 10 minutes, loosen cake from rim of pan. Cool completely; remove rim. Cover and chill cheesecake. Garnish with peanut butter cups, if desired. *Makes 10 to 12 servings*

banana nut cake with brown sugar topping

Carol Wright, Cartersville, GA

Cake
   3 bananas, mashed
1½ cups all-purpose flour
1½ cups packed brown sugar, divided
   ½ cup oil
   1 egg
   ¼ cup milk
   1 teaspoon baking soda
   1 cup chopped nuts
   ½ cup white baking chips

Topping
1⅔ cups packed brown sugar
   ½ cup (1 stick) butter
   ½ cup chopped nuts

1. Preheat oven to 350°F. Grease and flour 1-quart casserole or soufflé dish. Set aside.

2. Combine all cake ingredients, except nuts and baking chips, in large bowl; beat 2 minutes at medium speed with electric mixer until well blended. Stir in nuts and chips. Pour into prepared dish. Bake 30 to 35 minutes.

3. Meanwhile, combine 1⅔ cups brown sugar and butter in medium saucepan. Cook and stir over medium heat until sugar dissolves and mixture is smooth. Remove cakes from oven. Immediately sprinkle with ½ cup nuts and pour brown sugar mixture over cake. Cool completely on wire rack.

Makes 12 to 15 servings

cookies 'n' cream cake

Cindy Colby, Park Ridge, IL

  1 package (about 18 ounces) white cake mix
  1 package (4-serving size) white chocolate-flavored instant pudding and pie filling mix
  1 cup vegetable oil
  4 egg whites
  ½ cup milk
 20 chocolate sandwich cookies, coarsely chopped
  ½ cup semisweet chocolate chips
  1 teaspoon vegetable shortening
  4 chocolate sandwich cookies, cut into quarters for garnish

1. Preheat oven to 350°F. Spray 10-inch fluted tube pan with nonstick cooking spray.

2. Beat cake mix, pudding mix, oil, egg whites and milk 2 minutes in large bowl with electric mixer at medium speed or until ingredients are well blended. Stir in chopped cookies; spread into prepared pan.

3. Bake 50 to 60 minutes or until cake springs back when lightly touched. Cool 1 hour in pan on wire rack. Invert cake onto serving plate; cool completely.

4. Combine chocolate chips and shortening in glass measuring cup. Heat in microwave at HIGH (100%) 1 minute; stir. Continue heating at 15 second intervals, stirring, until melted and smooth. Drizzle glaze over cake and garnish with quartered cookies. *Makes 10 to 12 servings*

cookies 'n' cream cake

citrus cake

Etta Delores Faultry, Alvin, TX

      3 cups all-purpose flour
 2¾ cups sugar
      1 teaspoon baking powder
   ¼ teaspoon salt
 1¼ cups (2½ sticks) butter, softened
      5 eggs
   ⅔ cup milk
      1 teaspoon lemon extract
      1 teaspoon orange extract
         Citrus Cream Cheese Frosting (recipe follows)

1. Preheat oven to 350°F. Grease and flour 10-inch Bundt pan.

2. Combine flour, sugar, baking powder and salt in large bowl. Add butter, eggs and milk; beat 2 minutes at medium speed with electric mixer or until well blended. Stir in extracts. Pour batter into prepared pan.

3. Bake 50 to 60 minutes or until toothpick inserted near center comes out clean. Cool completely in pan on wire rack. Prepare Citrus Cream Cheese Frosting. Invert cake onto serving plate. Frost top and side of cake. Refrigerate 1 to 2 hours. *Makes 12 servings*

citrus cream cheese frosting

      1 package (8 ounces) cream cheese, softened
      1 container (8 ounces) frozen whipped topping, thawed
   ¼ cup sugar
      1 teaspoon orange extract
      1 teaspoon lemon extract

Combine all ingredients in bowl. Beat 2 minutes with electric mixer at medium speed until creamy.

devil's food cake

Sheryl Button, Cartersville, GA

2 cups sugar
1 cup shortening
1 cup buttermilk
2 eggs
3 cups all-purpose flour
1 cup unsweetened cocoa powder
1 package (4-serving size) chocolate-flavored instant pudding mix
1 cup hot water
½ cup oil
2 teaspoons vanilla
1 teaspoon salt
Powdered sugar, for garnish

1. Preheat oven to 375°F. Grease 10-inch Bundt pan. Set aside.

2. Beat sugar and shortening 3 minutes in large bowl with electric mixer at medium speed until light and fluffy. Add buttermilk and eggs; beat 1 minute or until blended.

3. Combine flour, cocoa and pudding mix in medium bowl. Add to sugar mixture, alternating with hot water and oil, beating until blended. Stir in vanilla and salt.

4. Pour batter into prepared pan. Bake 50 to 60 minutes. Cool in pan 30 minutes on wire rack. Invert onto serving plate. Cool completely. Sprinkle with powdered sugar.   *Makes 12 servings*

ganache-topped cheesecake

Carol Hartofil, Farmingdale, NY

4 packages (8 ounces each) cream cheese, softened
1 pint heavy cream
7 eggs
1½ cups sugar
2 tablespoons all-purpose flour
2 teaspoons vanilla
Chocolate Ganache (recipe follows)

1. Preheat oven to 350°F. Beat cream cheese and cream, a little at a time, 1 minute in large bowl with electric mixer at medium speed until smooth. Add eggs, one at a time, beating well after each addition. Add sugar, flour and vanilla; beat at low speed just until blended.

2. Pour mixture into ungreased 10-inch springform pan. Bake 50 to 60 minutes or until center appears set but still damp. Turn off oven but do not open door; allow to cool in oven for no more than 4 hours. Prepare Chocolate Ganache.

3. Remove side of springform pan; top with warm Chocolate Ganache, allowing chocolate to run down side of cake. Cover and refrigerate for 2 hours or until ready to serve.   *Makes 16 servings*

chocolate ganache

1 cup heavy cream
1 cup semisweet chocolate chips

Heat cream in small saucepan over medium-low heat until bubbles appear around edges of pan. Place chocolate chips in medium bowl. Pour cream over chips, stirring constantly, until mixture is smooth and begins to thicken. Keep warm. Mixture thickens and sets as it cools.

ganache-topped cheesecake

carrie's carrot cake

Carrie Martell, South Barre, VT

3 cups all-purpose flour
3 cups sugar
1 tablespoon baking soda
1 tablespoon ground cinnamon
1 teaspoon salt
1½ cups vegetable oil
4 eggs
1 tablespoon vanilla
1 can (20 ounces) crushed pineapple, well drained
1½ cups chopped walnuts
1⅓ cups blanched, drained grated carrots
¾ cup shredded coconut
Cream Cheese Frosting (recipe follows)

1. Preheat oven to 350°F. Grease three 9-inch round cake pans. Line bottoms with greased parchment paper. Set aside.

2. Combine flour, sugar, baking soda, cinnamon and salt in large bowl. Add oil, eggs and vanilla; beat 2 minutes with electric mixer at medium speed or until well blended.

3. Fold in pineapple, walnuts, carrots and coconut.

4. Pour mixture into prepared pans; bake 30 to 35 minutes or until knife inserted into centers comes out clean. Cool completely on wire rack.

5. Prepare Cream Cheese Frosting.

6. Place one cake layer on serving plate. Frost top of cake. Repeat layers using remaining cake layers and frosting. Frost side of cake. Refrigerate until ready to serve. *Makes 12 to 16 servings*

cream cheese frosting

1½ packages (8 ounces each) cream cheese, softened
½ cup plus 1 tablespoon butter, softened
1½ teaspoons vanilla
4½ cups powdered sugar

Beat cream cheese and butter in medium bowl with electric mixer at medium speed until smooth; add vanilla. Add powdered sugar, 1 cup at a time, beating well after each addition.

Carrie says: Blanching the carrots seems to make the cake moister (of course, adding the pineapple doesn't hurt either). This cake keeps well if refrigerated.

apple-peach dumpcake

Shannon Noelle Swatzell, Bellingham, WA

2 cans (20 ounces each) apple pie filling
2 cans (15 ounces each) sliced peaches, drained
1 teaspoon ground cinnamon, divided
½ teaspoon ground nutmeg, divided
1 package (about 18 ounces) white cake mix
¼ cup (½ stick) butter, melted

1. Preheat oven to 350°F. Place apple pie filling and peaches into 13×9-inch baking pan. Sprinkle with ½ teaspoon cinnamon and ¼ teaspoon nutmeg. Sprinkle cake mix on top of apple mixture.

2. Drizzle butter over top of cake mix. Sprinkle with remaining ½ teaspoon cinnamon and ¼ teaspoon nutmeg. Bake 1 hour or until top is lightly browned. Cool on wire rack. Serve warm or at room temperature.

Makes 12 to 15 servings

triple chocolate pudding cake

Jackie Schweitzer, Greenville, WI

  1 cup biscuit baking mix
½ cup sugar
¼ cup unsweetened cocoa powder
¾ cup milk, divided
⅓ cup butter, softened
  1 teaspoon vanilla
¾ cup hot fudge ice cream topping, divided
  1 cup semisweet chocolate chips, divided
¾ cup hot water or coffee
    Whipped cream or frozen whipped topping (optional)

1. Preheat oven to 350°F. Grease 8×8-inch pan.

2. Combine baking mix, sugar and cocoa in medium bowl. Beat in ½ cup milk, butter, vanilla and ¼ cup fudge topping until well blended. Stir in ½ cup chocolate chips. Pour batter into prepared pan.

3. Combine remaining ¼ cup milk, ½ cup fudge topping and hot water; stir until well blended. Pour over batter in pan. *Do not stir.* Sprinkle remaining ½ cup chocolate chips over fudge topping mixture.

4. Bake 45 to 50 minutes or until center is set. Cool 15 minutes on wire rack. Spoon pudding cake into dessert dishes. Serve with whipped cream, if desired. *Makes 8 servings*

yum-yum cake

Jackie Feinartz, Buffalo Grove, IL

1¼ cups granulated sugar divided
½ cup (1 stick) butter, softened
2 eggs
2 cups all-purpose flour
1 teaspoon baking soda
1 teaspoon baking powder
½ teaspoon salt
½ cup sour cream
½ cup milk
1 teaspoon vanilla
½ to 1 cup chopped pecans
⅓ cup packed brown sugar
1 teaspoon ground cinnamon

1. Preheat oven to 350°F. Grease 9×9-inch baking pan. Set aside.

2. Beat 1 cup granulated sugar and butter 2 minutes in large bowl with electric mixer at medium speed until fluffy. Add eggs, one at a time, beating well after each addition.

3. Sift flour, baking soda, baking powder and salt into medium bowl. Add flour mixture to butter mixture alternately with combined sour cream and milk, beginning and ending with flour, beating well after each addition until well blended. Stir in vanilla.

4. Combine pecans, remaining ¼ cup granulated sugar, brown sugar and cinnamon in medium bowl.

5. Pour half of batter into prepared pan; cover with half of cinnamon mixture; repeat with remaining butter and sugar mixture.

6. Bake 40 minutes or until toothpick inserted in center comes out clean.

Makes 10 to 12 servings

aunt lucille's chocolate pound cake

Rebecca J. Lacy, Claremore, OK

    3 cups all-purpose flour
    4 to 5 tablespoons unsweetened cocoa powder
    1 tablespoon baking powder
    ¼ teaspoon salt
    ½ cup (1 stick) margarine or butter, softened
    ½ cup shortening
    3 cups sugar
    4 eggs
    1 cup sweetened condensed milk
    1 teaspoon vanilla
       Chocolate Frosting (page 268)

1. Preheat oven to 300°F. Grease 10-inch Bundt pan. Set aside.

2. Sift flour into medium bowl. Sift again with cocoa, baking powder and salt. Beat margarine and shortening 1 minute in large bowl with electric mixer at medium speed. Gradually, beat in sugar. Add eggs, one at a time, beating well after each addition until blended. Add flour mixture, milk and vanilla, beating until blended. Pour into prepared pan.

3. Bake 1 hour or until toothpick inserted in center comes out clean. Cool cake completely in pan on wire rack. Invert cake onto serving plate.

4. Meanwhile, prepare Chocolate Frosting. Frost top and side of cake.

Makes 12 servings

continued on page 268

aunt lucille's chocolate pound cake

aunt lucille's chocolate pound cake, continued

chocolate frosting

¾ **cup sweetened condensed milk**
2 **squares (1 ounce each) unsweetened chocolate, chopped**
2 **cups sugar**
3 **to 4 tablespoons butter or margarine**
¼ **teaspoon salt**
1 **teaspoon vanilla**

Combine milk and chocolate in medium saucepan. Cook over low heat, stirring constantly, until almost thickened and chocolate is melted. Add sugar; bring to a boil. Boil 9 to 10 minutes, stirring constantly. Add butter and salt; remove from heat. Cool 20 minutes. Add vanilla; beat until spreadable.

Helpful Hint: **This frosting mixture is very hot. Take care not to splash it on your hands. Do not leave it unattended while it is boiling.**

neapolitan cheesecake

Lee Ann Camut, Warrington, PA

1¼ cups chocolate wafer or graham cracker crumbs
¼ cup (½ stick) butter, melted
3 packages (8 ounces each) cream cheese, softened
¾ cup sugar
1½ teaspoons vanilla
3 eggs
⅓ cup strawberry preserves
6 drops red food coloring
¾ cup white chocolate chips, melted
¾ cup semisweet chocolate chips, melted

1. Preheat oven to 350°F. Spray 9-inch springform pan with nonstick cooking spray.

2. Combine crumbs and butter in medium bowl. Press into bottom of prepared pan. Bake 9 minutes; cool.

3. Beat cream cheese, sugar and vanilla 2 minutes in large bowl with electric mixer at medium speed until well blended. Add eggs and beat until blended.

4. Divide batter equally into three medium bowls. Stir preserves and food coloring into one, white chocolate chips into second and semisweet chocolate chips into third. Spread semisweet chocolate mixture over crust. Repeat with preserves mixture, then white chocolate mixture.

5. Bake 1 hour or until center is almost set. Cool completely on wire rack. Refrigerate at least 3 hours. Carefully run knife around edge of pan to loosen. Remove side of pan. Serve immediately. Refrigerate leftovers.

Makes 8 to 10 servings

butterscotch malt zucchini cake

K. C. Hill, Siletz, OR

1¾ cups packed brown sugar
½ cup (1 stick) margarine or butter, softened
½ cup oil
2 eggs
½ cup buttermilk
1 teaspoon vanilla
2½ cups all-purpose flour
4 tablespoons malted milk powder
1 teaspoon baking soda
½ teaspoon salt
½ teaspoon baking powder
½ teaspoon ground nutmeg
2 cups grated zucchini
½ cup chopped nuts
½ cup butterscotch chips
½ cup white chocolate chips

1. Preheat oven to 350°F. Grease and flour 13×9-inch cake pan or 10-inch Bundt pan.

2. Beat brown sugar, margarine, oil and eggs 2 minutes in large bowl with electric mixer at medium speed. Add buttermilk and vanilla; beat until well blended.

3. Combine flour, milk powder, baking soda, salt, baking powder and nutmeg in medium bowl. Stir into creamed mixture just until blended. Stir zucchini, nuts, butterscotch chips and white chocolate chips into batter.

4. Pour batter into prepared pan. Bake 40 to 45 minutes (60 to 65 minutes for Bundt pan) or until toothpick inserted into center comes out clean. Cool completely on wire rack.

Makes 10 to 12 servings

lemon chiffon cake

Helen Fan, Cupertino, CA

      2 cups all-purpose flour
  1½ cups sugar
      1 tablespoon baking powder
      1 teaspoon salt
  ¾ cup cold water
  ½ cup vegetable oil
      2 teaspoons vanilla
      2 teaspoons grated lemon peel
      7 eggs, separated
      1 egg white
  ½ teaspoon cream of tartar
      Powdered sugar

1. Preheat oven to 325°F. Combine flour, sugar, baking powder and salt in large bowl. Beat in water, oil, vanilla, lemon peel and egg yolks with spoon until smooth.

2. Beat egg whites and cream of tartar in medium bowl with electric mixer on high speed until stiff peaks form. Fold egg whites into flour mixture until blended. Pour into ungreased 10-inch tube pan.

3. Bake 1¼ hours or until top springs back when lightly touched. Invert pan onto glass bottle or funnel. Cool completely. Remove from pan. Sprinkle with powdered sugar. *Makes 12 servings*

creamy coconut cake with almond filling

Donna Myers, Lewisville, NC

1 package (about 18 ounces) white cake mix
1 cup sour cream
3 eggs
½ cup vegetable oil
1 teaspoon vanilla
1 teaspoon coconut flavoring
1 can (12½ ounces) prepared almond filling
2 cans (16 ounces each) prepared creamy coconut frosting
½ cup sliced almonds

1. Preheat oven to 350°F. Spray two 9-inch round baking pans lightly with nonstick cooking spray and dust with 1 teaspoon flour. Tap pans to remove excess flour.

2. Combine cake mix, sour cream, eggs, oil, vanilla and coconut flavoring in large bowl. Beat 3 minutes with electric mixer at low speed until well blended. Divide evenly between prepared pans. Bake 30 to 35 minutes or until toothpick inserted into centers comes out clean. Cool completely in pans on wire racks.

3. Turn out cakes onto cutting board. Slice horizontally in half, making 4 layers. Place one layer cut side down on serving plate and spread with ½ almond filling. Top with second layer of cake and ½ cup coconut frosting. Top with third layer and remaining almond filling. Top with fourth cake layer; spread remaining coconut frosting over top and side of cake. Sprinkle with sliced almonds.

Makes 8 to 12 servings

Donna says: You can store this cake at room temperature, but I prefer to keep it refrigerated until ready to serve.

creamy coconut cake with almond filling

chocolate-peanut butter oatmeal snacking cake

Kelly Smarts, Sarasota, FL

1 cup uncooked old-fashioned oats
1¾ cups boiling water
1 cup granulated sugar
1 cup packed brown sugar
½ cup (1 stick) butter, softened
2 eggs, beaten
1 teaspoon vanilla
1¾ cups all-purpose flour
¼ cup unsweetened cocoa powder
1 teaspoon baking soda
1 cup semisweet chocolate chips
1 package (12 ounces) chocolate and peanut butter chips

1. Preheat oven to 350°F. Grease 13×9-inch baking pan; set aside.

2. Combine oats and boiling water in medium bowl; let stand 10 minutes. Add sugars and butter; beat 1 minute with electric mixer on low speed until well blended. Add eggs and vanilla; beat well.

3. Combine flour, cocoa and baking soda in medium bowl. Gradually beat into oat mixture until well blended. Stir in 1 cup chocolate chips. Pour into prepared pan. Sprinkle chocolate and peanut butter chips over top.

4. Bake 40 minutes. Cool completely in pan on wire rack.   *Makes 12 to 14 servings*

kentucky bourbon cake

Marie McConnell, Las Cruces, NM

4 cups all-purpose flour
2 teaspoons ground nutmeg
1½ teaspoons baking powder
3 cups chopped pecans
2 cups mixed candied fruit (about 1 pound)
2 cups raisins
2 cups orange marmalade
1½ cups (3 sticks) butter or margarine, softened
2 cups sugar
6 eggs
½ cup molasses
¾ cup bourbon

1. Preheat oven to 300°F. Line two 10-inch tube pans with waxed paper; grease well. Set aside.

2. Sift flour, nutmeg and baking powder into medium bowl; set aside. Combine pecans, candied fruit, raisins and marmalade in large bowl; add 1 cup flour mixture. Stir to coat well.

3. Beat butter and sugar 2 minutes in large bowl with electric mixer on medium speed until fluffy. Beat in eggs, one at a time. Stir in molasses. Add half remaining flour mixture, then bourbon, beating well after each addition. Beat in remaining flour mixture until well blended. Stir in fruit mixture. Pour into prepared pans.

4. Bake 2 hours or until toothpick inserted near centers comes out clean. Cool 10 minutes. Remove from pans to wire rack; cool completely. Wrap cakes in cheesecloth soaked with bourbon. Wrap in foil and let mellow for at least 2 days.   *Makes 12 servings*

Marie says: After a day or so you can sprinkle on an extra ¼ cup bourbon for more flavor.

delicious strawberry cake

Alexis Hitchman, Butler, OH

    4 eggs, separated
    1 package (about 18 ounces) yellow cake mix
1⅓ cups milk
    1 package (4-serving size) vanilla-flavored instant pudding mix
    ¼ cup oil
    1 teaspoon vanilla
      Icing (page 277)
    1 quart strawberries, stemmed and halved

1. Preheat oven to 375°F. Grease and flour two 9-inch round cake pans.

2. Beat egg whites in medium bowl with electric mixer at high speed until soft peaks form. Combine all remaining ingredients, except Icing and strawberries, in large bowl; beat 2 minutes with electric mixer at medium speed until well blended. Fold in egg whites.

3. Pour batter into prepared pans. Bake 28 to 32 minutes or until toothpick inserted into centers comes out clean.

4. Cool cakes 15 minutes in pans. Remove from pans to wire racks; cool completely.

5. Meanwhile, prepare Icing. Refrigerate until ready to use.

6. Cut cakes in half horizontally to make four layers. Place one layer on serving plate. Spread with Icing and top with strawberries. Repeat with remaining three cake layers, Icing and strawberries. Frost side of cake with remaining Icing. Garnish with remaining strawberries.

Makes 10 to 12 servings

icing

- 1 package (8 ounces) cream cheese, softened
- 1 container (8 ounces) frozen whipped topping, thawed
- 1 cup granulated sugar
- 1 cup powdered sugar
- ¼ cup margarine, softened
- 1 teaspoon vanilla

Combine all ingredients in small bowl. Beat with electric mixer at medium speed until smooth.

easy chocolate pudding cake

Brandy Richardson, Tuscon, AZ

- 1 package (6-serving size) chocolate-flavored pudding and pie filling mix
- 3 cups milk
- 1 package (about 18 ounces) chocolate fudge cake mix plus ingredients to prepare
  Whipped topping or ice cream (optional)

Slow Cooker Directions

1. Spray 4-quart slow cooker with nonstick cooking spray. Place pudding mix in slow cooker. Whisk in milk.

2. Prepare cake mix according to package directions. Carefully pour cake mix into slow cooker. *Do not stir.* Cover; cook on HIGH 2½ hours or until cake is set. Serve warm with whipped topping or ice cream, if desired.

Makes about 16 servings

blueberry yogurt cake

Bonnie R. Barter, Boothbay, ME

    1 cup applesauce
    ½ cup granulated sugar
    ¼ cup butter, softened
    2 eggs
    1 teaspoon vanilla
 1½ cups cake flour
    1 teaspoon baking powder
    ¼ teaspoon baking soda
    ½ cup plain or vanilla-flavored yogurt
    1 cup fresh blueberries
    1 cup chopped walnuts
    ½ cup packed brown sugar
    1 teaspoon ground cinnamon

1. Preheat oven to 350°F. Line 8-inch square baking pan with foil and spray with nonstick cooking spray.

2. Beat applesauce, granulated sugar and butter in medium bowl 2 minutes with electric mixer at medium speed. Beat in eggs and vanilla. Sift cake flour, baking powder and baking soda. Add to applesauce mixture with yogurt; beat until smooth. Flour berries and gently fold into batter.

3. Combine walnuts, brown sugar and cinnamon in small bowl. Sprinkle half of walnut mixture over bottom of prepared pan. Pour batter over walnut mixture. Sprinkle remaining walnut mixture over batter.

4. Bake 30 to 35 minutes or until toothpick inserted into center comes out clean. Cool 5 minutes. Remove from pan. Cool completely on wire rack. Garnish as desired.   *Makes 9 servings*

blueberry yogurt cake

raisin-nut cake

Jamie H. Mozingo, La Pine, OR

1 cup granulated sugar
¾ cup packed brown sugar
½ cup shortening
1 cup buttermilk
3 eggs
2 cups plus 2 tablespoons all-purpose flour
1 teaspoon baking powder
1 teaspoon salt
¾ teaspoon baking soda
½ cup chopped walnuts
½ cup raisins

1. Preheat oven to 350°F. Grease two 9-inch loaf pans. Set aside.

2. Beat sugars and shortening 2 minutes in large bowl with electric mixer at medium speed until light and fluffy. Beat in buttermilk and eggs.

3. Combine flour, baking powder, salt and baking soda in medium bowl. Gradually add flour mixture to sugar mixture, beating until well blended. Fold in walnuts and raisins. Pour into prepared pans.

4. Bake 1 hour or until toothpick inserted into centers comes out clean. Cool completely on wire rack.

Makes 2 loaves (12 to 16 servings each)

lemon cream cheese pound cake

Tena Camille DeAcklen, Chicago, IL

1⅔ cups cream cheese, softened
½ cup (1 stick) butter, softened
4½ teaspoons lemon extract
1 or 2 teaspoons yellow food coloring
5 eggs
5 packages (9 ounces each) single-layer yellow cake mixes
5 tablespoons all-purpose flour
1¼ teaspoons baking powder
4½ cups cold water

1. Preheat oven to 350°F. Grease and flour 10-inch tube pan. Cover bottom of pan with parchment or waxed paper trimmed to fit; grease paper. Set aside.

2. Combine cream cheese, butter, lemon extract and food coloring in large bowl. Beat 2 minutes with electric mixer until light and fluffy. Add eggs, one at a time, beating well after each addition. Add cake mixes, flour, baking powder and water; beat just until blended. Pour batter into prepared pan.

3. Bake 1 to 1½ hours or until toothpick inserted near center comes out clean. Cool completely in pan on wire rack.

Makes 16 servings

Tena says: This batter can also be used to make 3 (9-inch) loaf cakes. Reduce baking time to 35 to 40 minutes. You can also add raisins, chopped nuts or glacéed fruit dusted with flour. Freeze cake up to 6 weeks.

banana split roll

Trudi Hina, Zanesville, OH

3 eggs
1 cup sugar
2 medium bananas, mashed
1 teaspoon lemon juice
1 cup bread flour
2 teaspoons ground cinnamon
1 teaspoon baking powder
½ teaspoon salt
1 package (8 ounces) cream cheese, softened
1 cup powdered sugar
¼ cup (½ stick) butter, softened
⅓ cup crushed pineapple, well drained
½ teaspoon vanilla
1 cup semisweet chocolate chips
1 tablespoon shortening
1 cup chopped nuts (optional)

1. Preheat oven to 375°F. Grease and flour jelly-roll pan; set aside.

2. Beat eggs in large bowl 3 to 4 minutes with electric mixer at high speed until pale and thick. Gradually beat in sugar until blended. Beat in mashed bananas and lemon juice. Combine flour, cinnamon, baking powder and salt. Add flour mixture to egg mixture; beat on low speed just until blended. Pour into prepared pan.

3. Bake 15 minutes or until toothpick inserted near center comes out. Immediately turn cake onto towel dusted with flour. Starting on short side, roll up towel and cake. Place cake roll on wire rack; cool completely.

4. Beat cream cheese, powdered sugar, butter, pineapple and vanilla in medium bowl with electric mixer until smooth. Unroll cake and spread evenly with cream cheese mixture; roll up tightly. Wrap tightly in plastic wrap; refrigerate at least 30 minutes.

5. When ready to serve, melt chocolate chips and shortening in small saucepan over medium-low heat, stirring frequently. Drizzle thin ribbons of chocolate over cake. Immediately sprinkle with chopped nuts, if desired.   *Makes 8 servings*

golden creme cake

Ellen Parish, Boardman, OH

> 2 packages (10 cakes each) cream-filled golden snack cakes
> 2 containers (8 ounces each) frozen whipped topping, thawed
> 1 can (about 20 ounces) crushed pineapple, drained
> 3 bananas, cut into ¼-inch slices
> 1 package (4-serving size) vanilla instant pudding mix, prepared according to package directions
> 4 toffee candy bars (1½-ounces each), crushed and divided

1. Slice 10 snack cakes in half lengthwise and place, cut sides down, in single layer covering bottom of 13×9-inch baking dish. Top with one container whipped topping. Sprinkle with pineapple and banana slices; top with pudding. Sprinkle with half of toffee candy.

2. Slice remaining snack cakes in half lengthwise and place in single layer over toffee. Spread with remaining whipped topping and sprinkle with remaining toffee pieces.

3. Refrigerate 1 hour before serving.   *Makes 16 servings*

chocolate mint fluff roll

Jane Shapton, Tustin, CA

    4 eggs, separated
    ¾ cup granulated sugar, divided
    ½ cup (1 stick) butter, softened
    ¼ cup crème de menthe liqueur
    2 tablespoons water
    1 teaspoon vanilla
    ⅔ cup cake flour
    ½ cup unsweetened cocoa powder
    1 teaspoon baking powder
    ½ teaspoon salt
      Powdered sugar
      Chocolate Mint Filling (page 286)

1. Preheat oven to 375°F. Grease 15×10×1-inch jelly roll pan. Line with parchment paper and grease again; dust with flour.

2. Beat egg whites in large bowl with electric mixer at high speed until soft peaks form. Gradually add ½ cup granulated sugar, beating until egg whites are stiff and glossy. Set aside.

3. Combine egg yolks, remaining ¼ cup granulated sugar, butter, crème de menthe, water and vanilla in small bowl. Beat about 4 minutes or until mixture becomes thick. Fold yolk mixture into egg white mixture.

4. Sift flour, cocoa, baking powder and salt into medium bowl. Fold flour mixture into egg mixture until blended.

5. Pour batter into prepared pan. Bake 12 to 15 minutes or until edges begin to pull away from sides of baking pan and center springs back when lightly touched. Dust clean linen towel with powdered sugar. Invert cake onto towel. Peel off the parchment paper; start from long side and gently roll up cake. Cool cake completely. Prepare Chocolate Mint Filling.

continued on page 286

chocolate mint fluff roll

chocolate mint fluff roll, continued

6. Unroll cake; spread with filling. Roll up cake and place on serving plate. Sprinkle with additional powdered sugar. Chill before serving. *Makes 8 to 10 servings*

chocolate mint filling

- 1½ cups whipping cream
- ½ cup sugar
- ¼ cup unsweeted cocoa powder
- ½ teaspoon vanilla
- ¼ cup crème de menthe liqueur
- Pinch salt
- 1½ cups chopped chocolate mints

Beat cream, sugar, cocoa, vanilla, crème de menthe and salt in medium bowl on high speed with electric mixer until stiff peaks form. Gently fold in mints.

Helpful Hint: **This thin cake must be rolled, jelly-roll fashion while it is hot. Let the cake cool, then carefully unroll and spread with filling.**

pineapple-coconut cake

Peggy M. Gill, Allendale, SC

1 package (about 18 ounces) butter cake mix
¾ cup milk
½ cup (1 stick) butter, softened
3 eggs
½ teaspoon vanilla
1 can (20 ounces) crushed pineapple in heavy syrup, undrained
1 cup sugar
1 teaspoon cornstarch
2 cups shredded fresh coconut
1 container (8 ounces) sour cream
1 teaspoon coconut extract

1. Preheat oven to 325°F. Grease two 8-inch round cake pans.

2. Beat cake mix, milk, butter, eggs and vanilla in large bowl with electric mixer at medium speed until well blended. Pour batter into prepared cake pans.

3. Bake 25 to 30 minutes or until toothpick inserted into centers comes out clean. Cool 10 minutes. Remove to wire rack. Cool completely.

4. Combine pineapple with syrup, sugar and cornstarch in medium saucepan. Bring to a boil over low heat; remove from heat. Add coconut, sour cream and coconut extract; mix well.

5. Place one cake layer on serving plate. Spread coconut mixture on top of cake. Place remaining cake layer over coconut mixture. Spread top and side of cake with coconut mixture. Refrigerate until ready to serve.

Makes 10 servings

chocolate truffle torte

Marie McConnell, Las Cruces, NM

1½ cups milk
1 package (12 ounces) semisweet chocolate chips
6 squares (1 ounce each) unsweetened baking chocolate, chopped
1 cup packed brown sugar
1 container (8 ounces) pasteurized cholesterol-free egg substitute
2 teaspoons vanilla

1. Heat milk in medium saucepan over medium-low heat just until bubbles appear around edge of saucepan.

2. Combine chocolate chips, chopped chocolate and brown sugar in blender. Pour hot milk into blender; carefully blend until smooth. With blender running, add egg substitute and vanilla.

3. Pour chocolate mixture into 9-inch springform pan. Cover and chill at least 6 hours or overnight.

Makes 12 to 16 servings

Marie says: Serve with whipped cream and puréed strawberries or raspberries.

Helpful Hint: **Using pasteurized egg substitute will eliminate the risk of salmonella bacteria contamination in this torte. Do not substitute fresh eggs.**

chocolate truffle torte

apple cake

Shirley McLear, Manistique, MI

1¼ cups granulated sugar, divided
1 cup (2 sticks) margarine, softened
¾ cup packed brown sugar
2 eggs
1 teaspoon vanilla
1 cup buttermilk
2½ cups all-purpose flour
2 teaspoons ground cinnamon, divided
1 teaspoon baking powder
1 teaspoon baking soda
1 teaspoon salt
¼ teaspoon ground nutmeg
3 cups chopped apples
1 cup chopped nuts

1. Preheat oven to 350°F. Grease 13×9-inch pan. Set aside.

2. Beat ¾ cup granulated sugar, margarine, brown sugar, eggs and vanilla 3 minutes in large bowl with electric mixer at medium speed or until creamy. Beat in buttermilk.

3. Combine flour, 1 teaspoon cinnamon, baking powder, baking soda, salt and nutmeg in medium bowl. Beat into sugar mixture until well blended. Stir in apples.

4. Pour batter into prepared pan. Combine remaining ½ cup granulated sugar, remaining 1 teaspoon cinnamon and nuts in small bowl. Sprinkle over batter.

5. Bake 35 to 40 minutes or until toothpick inserted in center comes out clean. Cool completely on wire rack.

Makes 12 to 15 servings

double dutch choco-latte cheesecake

Lee Ann Camut, Warrington, PA

¼ cup butter, melted
2¾ teaspoons instant espresso powder or instant coffee, divided
1¼ cups chocolate wafer cookie crumbs
½ cup plus 2 tablespoons sugar, divided
2 packages (8 ounces each) cream cheese, softened
2 teaspoons vanilla
2 eggs
¼ cup unsweetened cocoa powder
¼ cup miniature semisweet chocolate chips
¼ cup chocolate-flavored syrup

1. Preheat oven to 350°F. Spray 9-inch springform pan with nonstick cooking spray.

2. Combine butter and 1½ teaspoons espresso powder in small bowl. Combine cookie crumbs and 2 tablespoons sugar in medium bowl. Add espresso mixture to cookie crumbs; stir until blended. Press into bottom of prepared pan; bake 9 minutes. Remove to wire rack; cool. *Reduce oven temperature to 325°F.*

3. Beat cream cheese, remaining ½ cup sugar and vanilla 2 minutes in large bowl with electric mixer at medium speed until well blended. Add 1 teaspoon espresso powder and eggs; beat until blended. Transfer half batter to another bowl and reserve. Add cocoa to remaining batter and beat at low speed until well blended. Pour over crust in prepared pan. Stir chocolate chips into reserved batter; pour over cocoa mixture.

4. Bake 40 minutes or until center is almost set. Remove to wire rack; cool completely. Cover and refrigerate for at least 3 hours. Run thin knife around edge of pan before removing sides.

5. Heat chocolate syrup in microwave at HIGH 15 seconds. Stir in remaining ¼ teaspoon espresso powder. Drizzle sauce over slices of cake just before serving. *Makes 8 servings*

ginger spice roll

Alicia Keller, Orwigsburg, PA

 3 eggs, separated
 ½ cup (1 stick) butter, softened
 ½ cup light molasses
 ¼ cup granulated sugar
 1 cup all-purpose flour
 ¾ teaspoon baking soda
 ½ teaspoon ground ginger
 ½ teaspoon ground cinnamon
 ½ teaspoon ground cloves
 ¼ teaspoon ground nutmeg
   Powdered sugar
   Spiced Filling (page 293)

1. Preheat oven to 375°F. Grease 15×10×1-inch jelly roll pan. Line pan with parchment paper and grease; dust pan with flour.

2. Beat egg yolks 4 minutes in large bowl with electric mixer at high until mixture is thick and lemon colored. Add butter and molasses; beat 1 minute.

3. Beat egg whites in small bowl until foamy. Add granulated sugar, beating until soft peaks form. Fold into egg yolk mixture. Sift flour, baking soda, ginger, cinnamon, cloves and nutmeg into small bowl. Fold into egg mixture until well blended.

4. Pour batter into prepared pan. Bake 10 to 12 minutes or until cake is golden and edges begin to pull away from sides of pan. Dust clean linen towel with powdered sugar. Remove pan from oven and invert cake onto towel. Peel off parchment paper; gently roll cake, starting from short side. Cool cake completely. Prepare Spiced Filling.

5. Unroll cake, spread with Spiced Filling; roll up cake. Sprinkle with additional powdered sugar. Serve with vanilla ice cream. *Makes 8 to 10 servings*

spiced filling

    1 package (8 ounces) cream cheese, softened
    ¼ cup butter
    1 cup powdered sugar
    ½ teaspoon vanilla
    ¼ teaspoon ground ginger
    ¼ teaspoon ground cinnamon

Beat cream cheese and butter. Stir in powdered sugar, vanilla and spices until smooth.

pineapple coconut pound cake

Brenda B. Melancon, Bay St. Louis, MS

    1 package (18¼ ounces) yellow cake mix
    1 package (4-serving size) cheesecake-flavored instant pudding mix
    1 can (8 ounces) crushed pineapple, undrained
    3 eggs
    ½ cup water
    ¼ cup vegetable oil
    1 cup shredded coconut
    Non-dairy whipped topping (optional)

1. Preheat oven to 350°F. Grease two 8×4×2-inch loaf pans.

2. Combine all ingredients except coconut and whipped topping in large bowl. Beat 2 minutes at medium speed with electric mixer. Stir in coconut. Pour into prepared pans.

3. Bake 45 to 50 minutes or until toothpick inserted into centers comes out clean. Cool 10 minutes in pans; remove to wire racks. Serve with whipped topping, if desired.   *Makes 24 servings*

root beer float cheesecake

James Morrow, Riverbank, CA

1½ cups shortbread cookie crumbs
2 tablespoons margarine, melted
4 packages (8 ounces each) cream cheese, softened
1 cup granulated sugar
1 teaspoon vanilla
4 eggs
1½ teaspoons root beer concentrate
1½ cups whipping cream
¼ cup plus 2 tablespoons powdered sugar

1. Preheat oven to 350°F. Combine crumbs and margarine; press into bottom of 9-inch springform pan.

2. Beat cream cheese, granulated sugar and vanilla 2 minutes in large bowl with electric mixer at medium speed until well blended. Add eggs; beat until blended.

3. Transfer 1¼ cups batter to small bowl. Add root beer concentrate; stir. Spoon half of cream cheese mixture into crust. Spoon half of root beer mixture over cream cheese mixture. Repeat layers. Swirl with knife or spatula to create marbled effect.

4. Bake 45 to 50 minutes or until center is almost set. Loosen cake from rim of pan; cool completely. Remove rim of pan. Chill.

5. Beat whipping cream in large bowl with electric mixer at high speed until thickened. (Chill bowl and beaters in freezer for best results.) Add powdered sugar. Beat at high speed until stiff peaks form. Spread over cheesecake. Refrigerate until ready to serve. *Makes 10 to 12 servings*

James says: You can substitute softened vanilla ice cream for the whipped cream.

root beer float cheesecake

chocolate rum cake

Tricia Bailey, Moody, AL

    1 cup chopped pecans
    1 package (12 ounces) semisweet chocolate chips
    1 package (8 ounces) cream cheese, softened
    1 package (about 18 ounces) yellow cake mix
    1 package (4-serving size) vanilla instant pudding mix
    5 eggs
    ½ cup oil
    ½ cup cold water
    3 tablespoons dark rum
    1 teaspoon vanilla
      Rum Butter Glaze (page 297)

1. Preheat oven to 325°F. Grease and flour 10-inch tube pan or 12-cup Bundt pan. Sprinkle chopped pecans onto bottom of pan.

2. Place chocolate chips and cream cheese in microwavable glass bowl. Heat in microwave at MEDIUM (50% power) 1 minute. Stir until smooth; set aside to cool.

3. Combine cake mix, pudding mix, eggs, oil, water, rum and vanilla in large bowl; mix until smooth. Add cream cheese mixture; blend well.

4. Pour batter into prepared pan. Bake 45 to 50 minutes or until toothpick inserted near center comes out clean. *Do not overbake.* Cool 15 minutes in pan on wire rack.

5. Prepare Rum Butter Glaze.

6. Spoon ½ glaze over cake. Invert cake onto serving platter. Brush remaining glaze over top and side of cake, using pastry brush. Wrap tightly in foil. *Makes 10 to 12 servings*

rum butter glaze

½ cup (1 stick) butter
1 cup sugar
¼ cup water
3 tablespoons dark rum
1 teaspoon vanilla

Melt butter in medium saucepan over low heat. Add sugar and water; boil 5 minutes, stirring often. Remove syrup from heat; let cool. Stir in rum and vanilla.

ice box fruit cake

Alana Simpson, Hokes Bluff, AL

1 package (12 ounces) vanilla wafers, finely crushed
1½ cups candied fruit mix
1 package (½ ounce) raisins
½ cup chopped pecans
1 can (14 ounces) sweetened condensed milk
Powdered sugar

1. Combine wafer crumbs, fruit mix, raisins and pecans in large bowl. Add milk and mix well.

2. Roll mixture in powdered sugar. Shape into wide log shape and place onto baking sheet. Refrigerate overnight. Cut into slices.

Makes 8 to 10 servings

lazy-daisy cake

Heidi Demeo, Long Grove, IL

   2 cups granulated sugar
   4 eggs
   2 teaspoons vanilla
   2 cups all-purpose flour
   2 teaspoons baking powder
   1 cup warm milk
   ½ cup (1 stick) butter, divided
   ½ cup plus 2 tablespoons brown sugar
   ⅓ cup half-and-half
   1 cup coconut flakes

1. Preheat oven to 350°F. Grease 13×9-inch baking pan.

2. Beat granulated sugar, eggs and vanilla 3 minutes in large bowl with electric mixer until fluffy. Sift flour and baking powder into medium bowl. Beat into egg mixture until well blended. Stir in milk and 2 tablespoons butter. Pour into prepared pan. Bake 30 minutes or until toothpick inserted in center comes out clean.

3. Meanwhile, combine brown sugar, half-and-half, remaining 6 tablespoons butter and coconut in medium saucepan over medium heat. Cook until sugar dissolves and butter melts, stirring constantly.

4. Spread coconut mixture over warm cake. Place under broiler, 4 inches from heat source. Broil 2 to 3 minutes or until top turns light golden brown.   *Makes 12 to 14 servings*

Tip: When broiling the topping, watch carefully to prevent burning.

cream cheese cupcakes

Laura T. Dowling, Belleville, NJ

3 packages (8 ounces each) cream cheese, softened
5 eggs
1¼ cups sugar, divided
1½ teaspoons vanilla
1 container (16 ounces) sour cream
1 teaspoon vanilla
1 cup fresh pitted cherries, fresh blueberries or crushed pineapple, drained

1. Preheat oven to 325°F. Line 24 (2½-inch) muffin cups with paper liners.

2. Beat cream cheese, eggs, 1 cup sugar and vanilla 2 minutes in large bowl with electric mixer on medium speed or until well blended.

3. Fill muffin cup ¾ full. Bake 20 minutes or until light golden brown. Remove from oven; cool 5 minutes. (Cupcakes will settle slightly.)

4. Combine sour cream, ¼ cup sugar and vanilla in medium bowl stir until blended. Fill depression in cupcakes with sour cream mixture. Bake 5 minutes more. Cool 10 minutes. Remove from pans and cool completely on wire racks.

5. Top cupcakes with desired fruit topping.   *Makes 24 cupcakes*

Helpful Hint: **Avoid overbeating cheesecake batter because this can contribute to surface cracking during cooling.**

cookie pizza cake

Lee Ann Camut, Warrington, PA

1 package (18 ounces) refrigerated chocolate chip cookie dough
1 package (16 to 18 ounces) chocolate cake mix, plus ingredients to prepare
1 cup vanilla frosting
½ cup peanut butter
1 to 2 tablespoons milk
1 container (16 ounces) chocolate frosting
   Chocolate peanut butter cups or other candy pieces (optional)

1. Preheat oven to 350°F. Coat two 12-inch round pizza pan with nonstick cooking spray. Press cookie dough evenly into one pan. Bake 15 to 20 minutes or until edges are golden brown. Cool 20 minutes in pan on wire rack. Loosen edge of cookie with knife. Turn pan over to release cookie. Set aside.

2. Prepare cake mix according to package directions. Fill second pan ¼ to ½ full with batter. (Reserve remaining cake mix for another use, such as cupcakes.) Bake 10 to 15 minutes or until toothpick inserted in center comes out clean. Cool 15 minutes on wire rack. Gently remove cake from pan to cool completely.

3. Combine vanilla frosting and peanut butter in small bowl. Gradually stir in milk, 1 tablespoon at a time, until of spreadable consistency.

4. Place cookie on serving plate. Spread peanut butter frosting on top of cookie. Place cake on top of cookie, trimming cookie to match the size of cake, if necessary. Frost top and side of cake with chocolate frosting. Decorate with peanut butter cups, if desired. Cut into slices.

Makes 12 to 14 servings

cookie pizza cake

easy banana sundae cake

Brenda Sue Davidson, Punta Gordon, FL

    2 ripe bananas
 1½ cups granulated sugar
    2 eggs
 1⅓ cups buttermilk
    ½ cup (1 stick) butter, melted
    3 cups self-rising flour
    2 teaspoons vanilla, divided
    2 cups whipping cream
    ½ cup powdered sugar
    1 can (21 ounces) strawberry pie filling
      Chocolate syrup

1. Preheat oven to 350°F. Grease two 9-inch round cake pans with nonstick cooking spray.

2. Beat bananas in large bowl with electric mixer at low speed. Add granulated sugar and eggs; beat until blended. Beat in buttermilk and butter. Add flour, 1 cup at a time, beating well after each addition. Add 1 teaspoon vanilla. Beat at medium speed 2 minutes. Spread into prepared pans.

3. Bake 30 minutes or until center springs back when lightly touched. Cool in pans 10 minutes. Remove from pans; cool completely on wire racks.

4. Beat whipping cream in medium bowl with electric mixer on high speed until very thick. Add remaining 1 teaspoon vanilla and powdered sugar; beat until blended.

5. Place one cake layer on serving plate. Frost top of cake with whipping cream mixture. Top with ½ can strawberry pie filling. Top with remaining cake layer. Frost top and side with remaining whipping cream mixture. Draw a circle around edge of cake with chocolate syrup. Fill circle with remaining strawberry pie filling. Cover and refrigerate until ready to serve.

Makes 10 to 12 servings

airy chocolate cake

Patricia Watkins, Liberty Hill, TX

2 cups all-purpose flour
1 cup (2 sticks) butter, melted
½ cup granulated sugar
1 cup chopped pecans
1 package (8 ounces) cream cheese
1 cup powdered sugar
2 containers (8 ounces each) frozen whipped topping, thawed
1 package (4-serving size) vanilla instant pudding mix
1 package (4-serving size) chocolate instant pudding mix
3 cups milk

1. Preheat oven to 350°F. Combine flour, butter and granulated sugar in medium bowl. Reserve 1 tablespoon pecans; set aside. Add remaining pecans to flour mixture. Press into 13×9-inch baking pan. Bake 20 minutes; cool completely.

2. Beat cream cheese and powdered sugar 2 minutes in medium bowl with electric mixer at medium speed until smooth. Fold in 1 cup whipped topping. Spread over pecan layer.

3. Combine pudding mixes in large bowl. Add milk; mix well. Spread over cream cheese layer.

4. Top pudding layer with remaining whipped topping and sprinkle with reserved 1 tablespoon pecans. Refrigerate 4 hours. *Makes 10 to 12 servings*

zucchini and apple pound cake

Jean Jackson, Columbus, GA

2¼ cups (4½ sticks) unsalted butter, softened
2¾ cups sugar
  5 eggs
  ¼ cup grated zucchini
  ⅓ cup applesauce
  ½ cup evaporated milk
  3 cups all-purpose flour
1½ teaspoons baking powder
  ½ teaspoon salt
  ¼ teaspoon baking soda
  ½ medium Golden Delicious apple, peeled and diced
  2 teaspoons vanilla
  1 teaspoon lemon juice
    Zucchini and Apple Frosting (page 305)
    Vanilla ice cream (optional)

1. Preheat oven to 350°F. Grease 10-inch tube baking pan.

2. Beat butter and sugar 3 minutes in large bowl with electric mixer on medium until pale and fluffy. Add eggs, one at a time, beating well after each addition. Stir in zucchini and applesauce.

3. Stir in evaporated milk; beat 2 minutes until well blended. Combine flour, baking powder, salt and baking soda. Add to butter mixture; mix well. Stir in apple, vanilla and lemon juice.

4. Pour batter into prepared pan. Bake 75 to 80 minutes or until toothpick inserted near center comes out clean. Cool in pan 15 minutes. Invert cake onto wire rack; cool completely. Prepare Zucchini and Apple Frosting; frost top and side of cake. Serve with vanilla ice cream, if desired.

Makes 10 servings

zucchini and apple frosting

1 package (16 ounces) powdered sugar
1 package (8 ounces) cream cheese, softened
½ cup (1 stick) butter
1 teaspoon vanilla
4 to 6 tablespoons milk
⅓ cup finely grated zucchini
½ Golden Delicious apple, peeled and diced

1. Beat sugar, cream cheese, butter and vanilla in medium bowl with electric mixer at medium speed until fluffy.

2. Beat in 2 tablespoons milk; stir in zucchini and apple. If frosting seems too thick, add more milk, 1 tablespoon at a time, until frosting is of spreadable consistency.

chocolate-raspberry layer cake

Janel M. Belbute, Haverhill, MA

2 packages (about 18 ounces each) chocolate cake mix, plus ingredients to prepare
1 jar (10 ounces) seedless red raspberry fruit spread, divided
1 package (12 ounces) white chocolate chips, divided
1 container (16 ounces) chocolate frosting
½ pint fresh raspberries
1 to 2 cups toasted slivered almonds

1. Preheat oven to 350°F. Grease and flour four 9-inch round cake pans. Prepare cake mixes according to package directions. Pour into prepared pans. Bake as directed on package. Cool 10 minutes. Remove cakes from pans. Cool cakes completely on wire rack.

2. Place one cake layer on serving plate. Spread with ⅓ of fruit spread. Sprinkle with ½ cup white chocolate chips.

3. Repeat with second and third layers, fruit spread and white chocolate chips.

4. Place fourth cake layer on top. Frost top and sides of cake with chocolate frosting. Decorate cake in alternating concentric circles of raspberries and remaining ½ cup white chocolate chips. Press almonds against side of cake. *Makes 8 to 10 servings*

Helpful Hint: **For easier spreading of fruit spreads, stir them before attempting to spread them on a cake.**

chocolate-raspberry layer cake

chocolate cinnamon cake

Cindy Colby, Park Ridge, IL

½ cup (1 stick) butter, softened
1½ cups sugar
2 eggs
1 teaspoon vanilla
¾ cup semisweet chocolate chips, melted and cooled
1¾ cups all-purpose flour
1 tablespoon ground cinnamon
2 teaspoons baking soda
¼ teaspoon salt
¾ cup buttermilk
½ cup vegetable oil
Chocolate Glaze (recipe follows)

1. Preheat oven to 350°F. Grease and flour 10-cup fluted tube pan. Beat butter and sugar 3 minutes in large bowl with electric mixer at medium speed until light and fluffy. Beat in eggs and vanilla until blended. Stir in chocolate.

2. Combine flour, cinnamon, baking soda and salt in medium bowl. Add flour mixture to butter mixture alternately with buttermilk and oil, beginning and ending with flour mixture. Beat well after each addition. Pour batter into prepared pan.

3. Bake 45 to 55 minutes or until cake begins to pull away from side of pan. Cool in pan 10 minutes. Remove from pan to wire rack; cool completely.

4. Prepare Chocolate Glaze; drizzle over cooled cake.   *Makes 10 to 12 servings*

Chocolate Glaze: Combine ½ cup semisweet chocolate chips and 1 teaspoon vegetable shortening in glass measuring cup. Heat in microwave at HIGH (100%) 1 minute; stir. Continue heating at 15 second intervals, stirring, until melted and smooth.

easy patriotic layer cake

Donna Abramchuk, Porterville, CA

1 container (16 ounces) low-fat ricotta cheese
¼ cup applesauce
2 tablespoons sugar
⅛ teaspoon vanilla
2 containers (8 ounces each) fresh blueberries, divided
2 containers (8 ounces each) fresh raspberries, divided
2 loaves (10 ounces each) prepared angel food cake

1. Combine ricotta, applesauce, sugar and vanilla in medium bowl. Combine ¼ cup blueberries and ¼ cup raspberries in small bowl; set aside.

2. Cut each cake into 10 slices. Line bottom and sides of 9-inch loaf pan with 11 slices of cake (3 on bottom, 3 on each long side and 1 at each end). Spoon about ¼ of ricotta mixture into pan, spreading over cake in even layer. Top with ½ remaining blueberries, then 3 slices cake. Spread with another ¼ of ricotta mixture. Top with remaining raspberries and 3 slices cake.

3. Spread cake with another ¼ of ricotta mixture; top with remaining blueberries and final 3 slices of cake. Top with remaining ricotta mixture and sprinkle with reserved mixed berries. Cover and refrigerate at least 1 hour before serving.

Makes 12 servings

Helpful Hint: **Ricotta cheese is a soft Italian cheese that resembles cottage cheese but it is smoother and creamer. It is readily available in large supermarkets.**

southern peanut butter cake

Mrs. Lucinda Blankenship, Hurley, VA

  2 cups sugar
  2 cups all-purpose flour
  1 cup peanut butter
  ½ cup (1 stick) butter or margarine, softened
  ½ cup peanut or vegetable oil
  5 eggs, separated
  2 teaspoons baking soda
  1 teaspoon vanilla
  1 can (3½ ounces) flaked coconut
    Cream Cheese Frosting (page 311)
  1 to 2 cups chopped roasted peanuts (optional)

1. Preheat oven to 350°F. Grease three 9-inch round cake pans. Set aside.

2. Combine sugar, flour, peanut butter, butter, oil, egg yolks, baking soda and vanilla in large bowl. Beat at medium speed until well blended; stir in coconut.

3. Beat egg whites in medium bowl with electric mixer at high speed until stiff peaks form. Fold into sugar mixture. Pour batter into prepared pans.

4. Bake 25 to 30 minutes or until toothpick inserted into centers comes out clean. Cool in pans 10 minutes. Remove to wire racks; cool completely.

5. Prepare Cream Cheese Frosting. Place one cake layer on serving plate. Frost top of cake. Repeat with remaining three layers and frosting. Frost side of cake. Sprinkle with chopped peanuts, if desired. Refrigerate until ready to serve.

Makes 8 servings

cream cheese frosting

1 package (8 ounces) cream cheese, softened
½ cup (1 stick) butter, softened
1 box (16 ounces) powdered sugar
1 teaspoon vanilla

Beat cream cheese and butter in medium bowl with electric mixer at medium speed until fluffy. Gradually add powdered sugar and vanilla. Beat until well blended.

butterscotch cake

Elizabeth Lewis, Evarts, KY

1½ cups self-rising flour
1 cup sugar
1 cup sour cream
1 package (4-serving size) butterscotch-flavored instant pudding mix
½ cup water
½ cup oil
4 eggs
1 bag (10 ounces) butterscotch chips

1. Preheat oven to 325°F. Grease 10-inch Bundt pan. Combine all ingredients except butterscotch chips in medium bowl; beat with electric mixer at medium speed until well blended. Fold in butterscotch chips.

2. Bake 45 to 60 minutes or until toothpick inserted near center comes out clean. Cool completely on wire rack. Remove from pan. *Makes 12 servings*

WINNING DESSERTS

cheesecake-filled strawberries

Gina Cramer, North Branch, MI

- 1 package (8 ounces) cream cheese
- 1½ tablespoons powdered sugar
- 1½ teaspoons vanilla
- 1 package (8 ounces) almonds, toasted
- 1 pint strawberries

1. Beat cream cheese 2 minutes in medium bowl with electric mixture at medium speed until creamy. Add powdered sugar and vanilla; beat until well blended. Transfer to pastry bag fitted with small round or star tip.

2. Wash but do not hull strawberries. Cut berries in half lengthwise, creating heart-shaped halves.

3. Pipe cream cheese mixture onto strawberries. Press 2 toasted almonds into cream cheese on each strawberry. Arrange berries on serving platter. Refrigerate until ready to serve.

Makes 6 to 8 servings

Tip: If you don't have a pastry bag, place the cream cheese mixture in a resealable plastic food storage bag. Seal it, then cut off the corner of the bag. Squeeze the bag and pipe the cream cheese mixture onto the strawberry halves.

cheesecake-filled strawberries

cookies and cream layered dessert

Phyllis Tatro, Springfield, MA

1 cup cold milk
1 package (4-serving size) white chocolate-flavored instant pudding mix
1 package chocolate creme-filled sandwich cookies
¼ cup butter, melted
2 packages (8 ounces each) cream cheese, softened
2 cups powdered sugar
1 container (8 ounces) frozen whipped topping, thawed
1 teaspoon vanilla
2 cups whipping cream

1. Combine milk and pudding mix in medium bowl; beat 2 minutes with wire whisk. Set aside.

2. Finely crush cookies in resealable plastic food storage bag with rolling pin or in blender. Combine 2 cups crushed cookies and butter in small bowl. Place on bottom of 2-quart trifle dish. Reserve remaining crushed cookies.

3. Beat cream cheese and powdered sugar 2 minutes in large bowl with electric mixer on medium speed until smooth. Fold in pudding mixture, whipped topping and vanilla.

4. Beat whipping cream in small deep bowl with electric mixer on high speed until soft peaks form. Fold into cream cheese mixture.

5. Spoon ⅓ cream cheese mixture over cookie crumbs in trifle dish. Sprinkle ⅓ cookie crumbs over cream cheese. Repeat layers twice using remaining cream cheese mixture and cookie crumbs. Refrigerate until ready to serve. *Makes 12 servings*

coconut crunch delight

Mary Livengood, Meyersdale, PA

1¼ cups flaked coconut
1 cup all-purpose flour
1 cup slivered almonds
½ cup (1 stick) margarine, melted
¼ cup packed brown sugar
2⅔ cups cold milk
1 package (4-serving size) vanilla-flavored instant pudding mix
1 package (4-serving size) toasted coconut-flavored instant pudding mix
2 cups whipped topping

1. Preheat oven to 350°F. Grease 13×9-inch baking pan. Set aside.

2. Combine coconut, flour, almonds, margarine and brown sugar in large bowl; mix well. Spread coconut mixture into prepared pan. Bake 25 to 30 minutes or until golden brown, stirring every 10 minutes to form coarse crumbs. Cool. Remove half of coconut mixture to small bowl. Press remaining half of mixture onto bottom of same pan.

3. Combine milk and pudding mixes in medium bowl; whisk 2 minutes or until thickened. Fold in whipped topping. Spoon pudding mixture over crumb mixture in pan. Top with remaining crumb mixture. Cover and refrigerate overnight.   *Makes 12 to 16 servings*

grilled peaches with raspberry sauce

Gina Cramer, North Branch, MI

    1 package (10 ounces) frozen raspberries, thawed
1½ teaspoons lemon juice
    3 tablespoons brown sugar
    1 teaspoon ground cinnamon
    1 tablespoon rum (optional)
    4 medium peaches, peeled, halved and pitted
    2 teaspoons butter
    Fresh mint sprigs (optional)

1. Combine raspberries and lemon juice in food processor fitted with metal blade; process until smooth. Chill in refrigerator.

2. Combine brown sugar, cinnamon and rum, if desired, in medium bowl; roll peach halves in mixture. Place peach halves, cut side up, on foil. Dot with butter. Fold foil over peaches, leaving head space for steam; seal foil. Grill over medium coals for 15 minutes.

3. To serve, spoon 2 tablespoons raspberry sauce over each peach half. Garnish with fresh mint sprig, if desired.

Makes 4 servings

Helpful Hint: **For luscious fruit desserts with the best flavor, always choose fully ripened in-season fruit.**

nested sweet chocolate mousse

Catherine Hite, St. Michaels, MD

     2 **egg whites**
  ⅛ **teaspoon salt**
  ⅛ **teaspoon cream of tartar**
  ½ **cup sugar**
  ½ **cup chopped pecans**
 1½ **teaspoons vanilla, divided**
     1 **package (12 ounces) German sweet chocolate**
     3 **tablespoons water**
     1 **cup whipping cream**

1. Preheat oven to 300°F. Grease 8-inch pie plate. Set aside.

2. Beat egg whites, salt and cream of tartar in large bowl with electric mixer on high speed until foamy. Add sugar, 2 tablespoons at a time, beating well after each addition. Continue to beat until stiff peaks form. Fold in nuts and ½ teaspoon vanilla.

3. Spoon egg white mixture into prepared pie plate and make a shallow well in center. Bake 50 to 55 minutes, or until meringue is solid and crisp but not brown. Cool completely.

4. Place chocolate and water in small saucepan over low heat; stir until melted. Add remaining 1 teaspoon vanilla. Cool until room temperature. Beat cream in small deep bowl with electric mixer at high speed until soft peaks form. Fold chocolate mixture into cream. Spoon into meringue; chill at least 1 hour before serving.

Makes 8 servings

caramel apple bread pudding with cinnamon cream

Beth Royals, Richmond, VA

1 package (12 ounces) frozen escalloped apples, thawed
8 eggs, lightly beaten
2 cups milk
2 cups half-and-half
1 cup granulated sugar
½ cup unsalted butter, melted
2 teaspoons baking powder
1½ teaspoons ground cinnamon, divided
1 teaspoon vanilla
1 loaf (16 ounces) challah or any sweet bread, cut into ¾-inch cubes
1 package (12¼ ounces) caramel ice cream topping
2 cups vanilla ice cream
   Additional vanilla ice cream, for garnish
   Mint sprigs, for garnish

1. Preheat oven to 350°F. Spray 13×9-inch baking pan with nonstick cooking spray.

2. Combine apples, eggs, milk, half-and-half, sugar, butter, baking powder, 1 teaspoon cinnamon and vanilla in large bowl. Mix well. Gently fold in bread cubes. Pour into prepared pan.

3. Bake 50 minutes or until set. Cool in pan 20 minutes.

4. Drizzle ½ cup caramel topping over bread pudding. Cut into 16 pieces.

5. Microwave ice cream in small bowl about 30 seconds or until partially melted. Stir until smooth. Add remaining ½ teaspoon cinnamon and whisk until blended. Place ⅛ of ice cream mixture on each serving plate. Top with serving of bread pudding. Drizzle each serving with ¼ cup caramel topping. Top with ice cream and mint sprig, if desired. *Makes 16 servings*

caramel apple bread pudding with cinnamon cream

angel food dream cake

Marguerite M. Campbell, Pittsburgh, PA

1 round angel food cake
2 cups milk
2 packages (4-serving size) vanilla-flavored instant pudding mix
1 container (8 ounces) frozen whipped topping, thawed
2 cans (21 ounces each) blueberry pie filling

1. Cut angel food cake into 1-inch cubes. Place in bottom of 11×7-inch pan.

2. Combine milk and pudding mixes in large bowl. Whisk 2 minutes until thickened. Fold in whipped topping. Pour over cake cubes. Top with pie filling. Chill overnight.

Makes 8 to 10 servings

eclaire dessert

Vikki Fry, Monterey, TN

3 cups milk
2 packages (4 serving size) vanilla instant pudding mix
1 container (8 ounces) frozen whipped topping, thawed
1 box (32 ounces) graham crackers
1 container (16 ounces) chocolate frosting

1. Beat milk and pudding mixes in large bowl with electric mixer. Beat 2 minutes until thickened. Fold in whipped topping.

2. Place ⅓ graham crackers in 13×9-inch baking dish. Top with ½ of pudding mixture. Repeat layers using ⅓ graham crackers and remaining pudding mixture. Top with remaining graham crackers. Spread frosting over graham crackers. Refrigerate at least 4 hours. *Makes 12 servings*

brownie pudding

Elaine Duesel, Marlboro, MA

    1 cup all-purpose flour
    ⅔ cup granulated sugar
    6 teaspoons unsweetened cocoa powder, divided
    2 teaspoons baking powder
    1 teaspoon salt
    ½ cup milk
    2 teaspoons shortening, melted
    1 teaspoon vanilla
    1 cup packed brown sugar
  1½ cups boiling water
      Vanilla ice cream

1. Preheat oven to 350°F. Grease 8×8-inch baking dish.

2. Sift flour, sugar, 2 teaspoons cocoa, baking powder and salt into large bowl. Add milk, shortening and vanilla; mix well. Pour into prepared pan.

3. Combine brown sugar and remaining 4 teaspoons cocoa in medium bowl. Sprinkle over batter. Pour water over brown sugar mixture. Bake 30 to 40 minutes. Serve warm with ice cream, if desired.

Makes 8 servings

Helpful Hint: For recipes that call for brown sugar, always choose the light brown variety unless the recipe specifically suggests dark brown sugar. Light brown sugar has a milder flavor than the more intense molasses flavor of dark brown sugar.

pumpkin bars

Jackie Remsberg, Carson City, NV

   4 eggs
1⅔ cups sugar
   1 can (16 ounces) solid packed pumpkin
   1 cup vegetable oil
   2 cups all-purpose flour
   2 teaspoons ground cinnamon
   2 teaspoons baking powder
   1 teaspoon baking soda
   1 teaspoon salt
1½ cups chopped pecans or walnuts, divided
   Cream Cheese Icing (page 323)

1. Preheat oven to 350°F.

2. Beat eggs in large bowl until well blended. Gradually add sugar, pumpkin and oil, beating well after each addition.

3. Sift flour, cinnamon, baking powder, baking soda and salt into medium bowl. Stir into pumpkin mixture. Fold in ½ cup pecans. Pour into ungreased 13×9-inch baking pan.

4. Bake 25 to 30 minutes or until toothpick inserted into center comes out clean. Cool completely in pan on wire rack.

5. Prepare Cream Cheese Icing.

6. Spread Cream Cheese Icing, over bars. Sprinkle with remaining 1 cup pecans. Cut into bars.

Makes about 18 bars

cream cheese icing

2 packages (3 ounces each) cream cheese, softened
2 tablespoons butter or margarine, softened
1 teaspoon vanilla
2 cups powdered sugar
1 to 2 tablespoons milk

Beat cream cheese 1 minute in large bowl with electric mixer on medium speed until fluffy. Add butter and vanilla; beat until blended. Add powdered sugar, ½ cup at a time, beating well after each addition. Stir in milk until icing is of spreading consistency. Refrigerate until ready to use.

cheesecake dessert

Tammy Reigle, Moncks Corner, SC

3 cups milk
2 packages (4-serving size each) cheesecake-flavored instant pudding mix
1 cup powdered sugar
2 containers (8 ounces each) frozen whipped topping, thawed
1 package (32 ounces) graham crackers
1 can (21 ounces) cherry pie filling

1. Combine milk, pudding mix, powdered sugar and 1 container whipped topping in large bowl; beat until blended. Set aside.

2. Grease 11×8-inch pan. Line pan with graham crackers. Spread half of pudding mixture over crackers and top with another layer of graham crackers. Repeat layers with remaining pudding mixture and graham crackers. Spread remaining container of whipped topping over last layer of graham crackers. Top with pie filling. Refrigerate 4 hours or overnight. *Makes 10 servings*

spicy raisin, date & candied ginger cobbler

Jim Lankford, Fredericksburg, VA

⅔ cup granulated sugar
2 tablespoons cornstarch
2 cups seedless raisins
1 cup chopped pitted dates
1 cup orange juice
⅓ cup water
2 tablespoons finely chopped candied ginger
3 tablespoons butter, divided
1 tablespoon lemon juice
½ teaspoon salt
1 small seedless orange, peeled, quartered and thinly sliced
1 can (10 ounces) flaky biscuits
2 tablespoons packed brown sugar
   Whipped cream (optional)

1. Preheat oven to 450°F. Combine sugar and cornstarch in large saucepan. Stir in raisins, dates orange juice, water and ginger. Bring to a simmer over medium heat, stirring constantly, until just thickened. Remove from heat. Stir in 1 tablespoon butter, lemon juice and salt. Fold in orange slices. Pour into 2-quart casserole dish.

2. Split biscuits in half horizontally. Cover top of raisin mixture with biscuit halves. Melt remaining 2 tablespoons butter. Brush butter onto biscuits. Sprinkle biscuits with brown sugar. Bake 10 minutes. *Reduce oven temperature to 350°F.* Bake 15 to 20 minutes or until biscuits are golden brown. Cool on wire rack. Serve warm or at room temperature with whipped cream, if desired.

Makes 8 to 10 servings

spicy raisin, date & candied ginger cobbler

chocolate heaven on earth

Zita Wilensky, Miami, FL

1¼ cups graham cracker crumbs
¾ cup plus 3 tablespoons sugar, divided
3 tablespoons unsweetened cocoa powder
¼ teaspoon ground cinnamon, divided
⅓ cup butter, melted
½ cup toasted sliced almonds, divided
1½ packages (8 ounces each) cream cheese, softened
2 eggs
1 tablespoon vanilla
1 tablespoon Tia Maria liquor (optional)
1 container (8 ounces) sour cream
1 square (1 ounce) semisweet chocolate, grated
1 square (1 ounce) white chocolate, grated
Mocha Topping (page 327)
Whipping cream

1. Preheat oven to 350°F.

2. Combine cracker crumbs, 3 tablespoons sugar, cocoa and ⅛ teaspoon cinnamon in medium bowl. Stir in butter. Press crumb mixture into 9-inch pie plate. Bake 8 minutes. Sprinkle with ¼ cup almonds.

3. Beat cream cheese and remaining ¾ cup sugar 2 minutes in large bowl with electric mixer at medium speed until fluffy. Beat in eggs, vanilla, liquor, if desired, and remaining ⅛ teaspoon cinnamon until well blended. Pour into prepared crust. Bake 30 minutes. Cool 15 minutes.

4. Spread sour cream on top of pie. Sprinkle with grated chocolates. Refrigerate.

5. Prepare Mocha Topping.

6. Pour Mocha Topping over pie. When ready to serve, beat whipping cream in medium bowl with electric mixer at high speed until stiff peaks form. Spoon over pie and sprinkle with remaining ¼ cup almonds.

Makes 8 to 10 servings

mocha topping

   1½ **teaspoons instant coffee granules**
    2 **tablespoons hot water**
    4 **squares (1 ounce each) semisweet chocolate**
    4 **egg yolks**
   ⅓ **cup sugar**
   ½ **teaspoon vanilla**

Dissolve coffee granules in water in medium saucepan over medium-low heat. Add chocolate; stir until melted. Cool slightly. Beat egg yolks 2 minutes in medium bowl with electric mixer at medium speed. Gradually add sugar, beating until sugar is dissolved. Stir in chocolate mixture and vanilla.

Helpful Hint: **Be sure to melt chocolate over medium-low heat, stirring constantly, until just melted. Remove from heat and let it cool slightly. If the chocolate mixture is too hot when it is added to the egg mixture, the egg mixture may curdle.**

ginger-peachy crisp

Marilyn Pocius, Oak Park, IL

 5 cups fresh peach slices
 ¼ to ½ cup granulated sugar
 ¾ cup uncooked old-fashioned oats
 ¾ cup packed brown sugar
 ½ cup all-purpose flour
 2 tablespoons finely chopped crystallized ginger
 ¼ teaspoon ground nutmeg
 ¼ cup butter, cut into chunks

1. Preheat oven to 350°F. Grease 8×8-inch baking dish; set aside.

2. Combine peach slices and ¼ cup granulated sugar in medium bowl. Add more sugar if peaches are not sweet enough.

3. Combine oats, brown sugar, flour, ginger and nutmeg in medium bowl. Cut butter into mixture using pastry blender or two knives until coarse crumbs form. Pour peach mixture into prepared pan. Sprinkle oat mixture over peaches.

4. Bake 20 to 30 minutes or until topping is crisp.   *Makes 6 to 8 servings*

Helpful Hint: **Crystallized ginger, sometimes called candied ginger, has been cooked in a sugar syrup and coated with coarse sugar. Look for it at large supermarkets or Asian markets.**

apple pita

Emily Hale, Chicago, IL

½ cup sugar
1 tablespoon cornstarch
1 teaspoon ground cinnamon
5 medium Macintosh apples, peeled and chopped
¾ cup (1½ sticks) butter
1 package (16 ounces) frozen phyllo dough, thawed
Vanilla ice cream (optional)

1. Preheat oven to 350°F. Grease 15×10-inch baking pan. Set aside.

2. Combine sugar, cornstarch and cinnamon in large bowl. Add apples and toss to coat.

3. Microwave butter in microwavable bowl at HIGH in 30 second increments until melted.

4. Unroll phyllo dough and cover with damp towel. Place 1 sheet phyllo dough in prepared pan. Using pastry brush, lightly coat phyllo dough with melted butter. Place 3 more sheets of phyllo dough on top of first sheet, brushing each with melted butter. Place apple mixture on top of phyllo. Repeat layers of phyllo dough on top of apple mixture using 4 sheets of phyllo dough, brushing each with melted butter.

5. Bake 40 minutes or until golden brown. Serve warm with ice cream, if desired.

Makes 10 to 12 servings

nancy's tiramisu

Nancy Minor, Phoenix, AZ

   6 **egg yolks**
1¼ **cups sugar**
1½ **cups mascarpone cheese**
1¾ **cups whipping cream, whipped to soft peaks**
1¾ **cups cold espresso or strong brewed coffee**
   3 **tablespoons brandy**
   3 **tablespoons grappa**
   4 **packages (3 ounces each) ladyfingers**
   2 **tablespoons unsweetened cocoa powder, divided**
     Whipped cream, for garnish (optional)
     Chocolate-covered espresso beans for garnish (optional)

1. Beat egg yolks and sugar in small bowl with electric mixer on medium-high speed until fluffy and pale yellow. Place in top of double boiler over boiling water. Reduce heat to low; cook, stirring constantly, 10 minutes. Combine yolk mixture and mascarpone cheese in large bowl; beat with electric mixer at low speed until well blended and fluffy. Fold in whipped cream. Set aside.

2. Combine espresso, brandy and grappa in medium bowl. Dip 24 ladyfingers individually into espresso mixture and arrange side-by-side in single layer in 13×9-inch glass baking dish. Dip ladyfingers into mixture quickly or they will absorb too much liquid and fall apart.

3. Spread ladyfinger layer evenly with half of mascarpone mixture. Sift 1 tablespoon cocoa over marscarpone layer. Repeat with another layer of 24 ladyfingers dipped in espresso mixture. Cover with remaining mascarpone mixture. Sift remaining 1 tablespoon cocoa over top.

continued on page 332

nancy's tiramisu

nancy's tiramisu, continued

4. Refrigerate at least 4 hours, but preferably overnight, before serving. Cut into slices to serve. Decorate with whipped cream and chocolate-covered espresso beans, if desired.

Makes 12 servings

Tip: If marscapone cheese is unavailable, combine 1 package (8 ounces) softened cream cheese, ¼ cup sour cream and 2 tablespoons whipping cream in medium bowl. Beat 1 minute with electric mixer on medium speed until light and fluffy.

lemon gingerbread trifle

Stephanie Overman, Chatham, NJ

> 1 package (14½ ounces) gingerbread mix, plus ingredients to prepare mix
> 1 package (4-serving size) lemon-flavored instant pudding mix, plus ingredients to prepare mix
> 3 tablespoons sherry
> ¼ cup raspberry or strawberry preserves
> 2 cups raspberries or sliced strawberries
> 2 tablespoons toasted sliced almonds
> 1 container (8 ounces) frozen whipped topping, thawed

1. Prepare and bake gingerbread mix according to package directions; cool completely.

2. Prepare and bake gingerbread mix according to package directions.

3. Cut gingerbread into 1-inch cubes. Layer half of the cake cubes in 2-quart serving bowl. Sprinkle with half of sherry. Layer 2 tablespoons preserves, 1 cup fruit and 1 tablespoon almonds over cake cubes. Spread ½ of pudding over fruit. Repeat layers using remaining cake cubes, sherry, preserves, fruit, almonds and pudding. Cover and chill 4 hours or overnight. Spread whipped topping over pudding just before serving.

Makes 8 servings

pumpkin flan

Marie McConnell, Las Cruces, NM

1 can (16 ounces) solid pack pumpkin
1 can (12 ounces) evaporated milk
1⅔ cups granulated sugar, divided
3 eggs, beaten
2 teaspoons vanilla, divided
1 teaspoon ground cinnamon
½ teaspoon ground ginger
½ teaspoon ground cloves
½ teaspoon ground nutmeg
¼ cup whipping cream
1 tablespoon powdered sugar

1. Preheat oven to 300°F. Beat pumpkin, evaporated milk, ⅓ cup granulated sugar, eggs, 1 teaspoon vanilla and spices in large bowl with electric mixer at medium speed until well blended. Set aside.

2. Heat remaining 1⅓ cups granulated sugar in large saucepan over medium-high heat, stirring until melted and golden brown. (Mixture will be very hot.) Carefully pour sugar into eight 4-ounce ramekins. Place ramekins into 15×11-inch baking dish and fill each cup with pumpkin mixture.

3. Pour hot water into pan until filled half way up sides of cups. Bake 45 to 55 minutes or until knife inserted in centers comes out clean. Remove from oven; cool. Run knife around edges of each cup to loosen. Invert onto serving plates.

4. Beat whipping cream, powdered sugar and remaining 1 teaspoon vanilla in small bowl with electric mixer at high speed until soft peaks form. Garnish each flan with whipped cream mixture.

Makes 8 servings

chocolate mint eclair dessert

Marie McConnell, Las Cruces, NM

23 whole chocolate graham crackers
3 cups cold reduced-fat (2%) or fat-free (skim) milk
2 packages (4-serving size) white chocolate- or vanilla-flavored instant pudding mix
½ teaspoon mint or peppermint extract
3 to 4 drops green food coloring (optional)
1 container (8 ounces) frozen reduced-fat whipped topping, thawed
   Cocoa Frosting (recipe follows)

1. Grease 13×9-inch baking dish with nonstick cooking spray. Line bottom of pan with three cracker halves and six whole crackers. Set aside.

2. Whisk milk and pudding mixes 2 minutes in large bowl until thickened. Whisk in extract and food coloring, if desired. Fold in whipped topping. Spread half of pudding mixture over graham crackers. Top with 3 graham cracker halves and 6 whole crackers. Spread remaining pudding mixture over crackers. Repeat graham cracker layer. Cover and refrigerate 2 hours.

3. Prepare Cocoa Frosting.

4. Spread Cocoa Frosting over graham crackers. Refrigerate until ready to serve.

Makes 12 to 14 servings

cocoa frosting

1 tablespoon butter
2 tablespoons unsweetened cocoa powder
2 tablespoons plus 1 teaspoon reduced-fat (2%) or fat-free (skim) milk
1 cup powdered sugar
1 teaspoon vanilla

Melt butter in small saucepan. Stir in cocoa and milk until blended. Remove from heat; stir in powdered sugar and vanilla.

tammy's triple banana treat

Tammy Reigle, Moncks Corner, SC

3 cups milk
1 cup powdered sugar
2 containers (8 ounces each) frozen whipped topping, thawed
2 packages (4-serving size each) banana-flavored instant pudding mix
1 box (32 ounces) graham crackers
6 bananas
½ cup chopped walnuts

1. Combine milk, powdered sugar, 1 container whipped topping and pudding mix in large bowl. Whisk 2 minutes until thickened.

2. Lightly grease 11×8-inch pan. Line pan with ⅓ of graham crackers.

3. Pour half of pudding mixture over crackers. Cut 2 bananas into slices. Place slices over pudding. Repeat layers using ⅓ of graham crackers, remaining pudding mixture and 2 sliced bananas. Place remaining ⅓ graham cracker over banana layer. Spread remaining 1 container whipped topping over graham crackers.

4. Slice remaining 2 bananas and place on top of whipped topping. Sprinkle with walnuts.

5. Refrigerate at least 4 hours or overnight.   *Makes 10 to 12 servings*

quick berry trifle

Julie Bottrell, Canyon Lake, CA

2 cups strawberry slices
1 cup fresh raspberries or blackberries
1 cup fresh blueberries
¼ cup sugar
1 pound cake (about 12 ounces), cut into ½-inch-thick slices
1 container (28 ounces) prepared vanilla pudding
1 can (7 ounces) aerosol whipped topping

1. Combine berries and sugar in medium bowl, stirring gently until blended.

2. Place single layer of cake slices in bottom of deep serving bowl. Top with ⅓ of pudding, then ⅓ of berries. Repeat layers twice, using remaining ingredients. Cover tightly with plastic wrap and refrigerate for at least 1 hour or until ready to serve.

3. Just before serving, remove from refrigerator. Top with whipped topping. Serve as desired.

Makes 12 servings

Helpful Hint: **This trifle is a good choice for an easy summertime dessert when berries are readily available and less expensive.**

quick berry trifle

german chocolate dessert

Dorothy Marihart, Graceville, MN

    2 cups graham cracker crumbs
    ½ cup ground pecans
    ¼ cup plus 2 tablespoons sugar, divided
    6 tablespoons butter, melted
    2 packages (4 ounces each) German sweet chocolate
    ⅓ cup milk
    1 package (8 ounces) cream cheese
    2 teaspoons vanilla
    1 container (12 ounces) frozen whipped topping, thawed

1. Combine graham cracker crumbs, pecans, ¼ cup sugar and butter in medium bowl. Press crumb mixture into bottom and up sides of 13×9-inch cake pan. Freeze 20 minutes.

2. Combine chocolate, milk and remaining 2 tablespoons sugar in large microwavable bowl. Microwave at HIGH 2½ to 3 minutes or until chocolate is almost melted; stir until smooth. Add cream cheese and vanilla; mix well. Cool completely. Fold in whipped topping.

3. Spoon chocolate mixture over crust; cool. Refrigerate 4 hours or overnight.

Makes 10 servings

california gold rush rice pudding

Lois Dowling, Tacoma, WA

2 cans (12 ounces each) orange soda
1 cup arborio rice
½ cup diced dried apricots
1 teaspoon butter
¼ teaspoon salt
½ cup chopped dates
⅓ cup toasted sliced honey roasted almonds
3 cups frozen whipped topping, thawed

1. Combine soda, rice, apricots, butter and salt in large saucepan. Bring to boil over medium-high heat, stirring frequently. Reduce heat. Cover and simmer 25 to 30 minutes or until liquid is absorbed. Remove from heat; cool.

2. Fold in dates and almonds. Refrigerate. Top with whipped topping before serving.

Makes 6 servings

strawberry delight

Judy C. Gibson, Pikeville, KY

1 container (12 ounces) frozen whipped topping, thawed
1 cup chopped pecans
1 cup strawberry pie filling
1 can (8 ounces) crushed pineapple, drained
1 cup sweetened condensed milk

Combine all ingredients in large bowl. Cover and refrigerate 3 to 4 hours. Serve in individual serving dishes.

Makes 4 servings

perfect peanut butter pudding

Lauren Silverman, Skokie, IL

> 2 cups milk
> 2 eggs
> ⅓ cup creamy peanut butter
> ¼ cup packed brown sugar
> ¼ teaspoon vanilla
> ¾ cup shaved chocolate or shredded coconut (optional)

1. Preheat oven to 350°F. Grease six (3-ounce) ovenproof custard cups; set aside.

2. Combine milk, eggs, peanut butter, brown sugar and vanilla in blender; process on high 1 minute. Pour into prepared custard cups. Place cups in 13×9-inch baking pan; add enough hot water to come halfway up sides of custard cups.

3. Bake 50 minutes or until pudding is set. Remove from oven, then remove custard cups from pan; cool slightly. Refrigerate until serving.

4. Just before serving, top each cup with about ⅛ cup shaved chocolate or shredded coconut, if desired.

Makes 6 servings

warm apple & blueberry crisp

Sheri Culler, Lucas, OH

6 medium apples, peel and cut into cubes
2 cups frozen blueberries
½ cup packed brown sugar, divided
¼ cup orange juice
½ cup buttermilk baking mix
½ cup uncooked old-fashioned oats
¼ cup butter, cut into pieces
¼ teaspoon ground cinnamon
¼ teaspoon ground ginger

1. Preheat oven to 375°F. Spray 9-inch square or round baking pan with nonstick cooking spray. Set aside.

2. Combine apples, blueberries, ¼ cup brown sugar and orange juice in medium bowl. Transfer to prepared pan.

3. Combine baking mix, oats, remaining ¼ cup sugar, butter, cinnamon and ginger in small bowl. Mix until coarse crumbs form. Sprinkle mixture evenly over fruit. Bake 45 minutes or until apples are tender.

Makes 6 servings

Helpful Hint: **If you keep frozen blueberries on hand you can make this delicious crisp any time of the year. There's no need to thaw the blueberries before using them.**

five-layer brownie dessert

Janine Stidley, Savannah, GA

1 package (19 to 21 ounces) chocolate brownie mix, plus ingredients to prepare
1 package (4-serving size) chocolate-flavored instant pudding mix, plus milk to prepare
1 package (8 ounces) cream cheese, softened
4 to 5 cups powdered sugar
2 cups (12 ounces) milk chocolate chips, divided
1 container (8 ounces) frozen whipped topping, thawed

1. Prepare brownie mix according to package directions for 13×9-inch pan. Set aside.

2. Prepare pudding mix according to package directions; set aside.

3. Combine cream cheese and powdered sugar in medium bowl; beat 1 minute with electric mixer at medium speed. Set aside.

4. Sprinkle prepared brownies with 1½ cups chocolate chips. Evenly spread cream cheese mixture over chocolate chips. Spread pudding mixture over cream cheese mixture. Spread whipped topping over pudding mixture. Sprinkle remaining ½ cup chocolate chips over whipped topping. Refrigerate until ready to serve. *Makes 12 to 14 servings*

five-layer brownie dessert

mom's heavenly berry cake

Loralee K. Pillsbury, Fort Carson, CO

1 package (4-serving size) sugar-free strawberry- or raspberry-flavored gelatin mix, plus water to prepare
1 angel food cake
1 package (4-serving size) vanilla-flavored pudding mix, plus milk to prepare
1 quart strawberries, stemmed and halved
¼ cup slivered almonds

1. Prepare gelatin mix according to package directions. Refrigerate 1 hour.

2. Meanwhile, crumble angel food cake into 13×9-inch baking dish. Prepare pudding according to package directions.

3. Pour gelatin mixture over cake. Place half of strawberries on cake. Spread pudding over strawberries. Sprinkle with almonds. Garnish with remaining strawberries. Refrigerate at least 1 hour or until ready to serve.

Makes 12 servings

Loralee says: You can substitute any kind of berries, nuts or pudding flavors in this recipe.

lemon layered dessert

Heather Samples, Cumming, GA

1 cup all-purpose flour
½ cup chopped nuts
½ cup (1 stick) butter
1 container (12 ounces) frozen whipped topping, thawed and divided
1 cup powdered sugar
1 package (8 ounces) cream cheese, softened
2½ cups milk
2 packages (4-serving size) lemon-flavored instant pudding

1. Preheat oven to 350°F. Combine flour and nuts in medium bowl. Cut in butter with pastry blender or two knives until mixture resembles coarse crumbs. Press into bottom of 13×9-inch baking pan. Bake 10 minutes. Cool completely.

2. Beat 2 cups whipped topping and powdered sugar in medium bowl with electric mixer until smooth. Spread over crust.

3. Combine milk and pudding mix. Whisk 2 minutes until thickened. Spread over cream cheese layer. Spread remaining whipped topping over pudding. Refrigerate until ready to serve.

Makes 12 to 16 servings

sugar loaf luau bread pudding with rum raisin sauce

Elaine Sweet, Dallas, TX

2 cups granulated sugar
2 cups whipping cream
1 can (15 ounces) cream of coconut
1½ cups toasted pistachios, coarsely chopped
1 cup shredded coconut, toasted
1 can (8 ounces) crushed pineapple in syrup, undrained
3 eggs, lightly beaten
½ cup (1 stick) butter, melted
2 tablespoons vanilla
1 teaspoon ground cinnamon
½ teaspoon ground cardamom
1½ loaves day-old French bread, crusts removed and bread cubed
Rum Raisin Sauce (page 347)
Powdered sugar (optional)

1. Preheat oven to 350°F. Spray deep 3-quart casserole with nonstick cooking spray.

2. Combine granulated sugar, whipping cream, cream of coconut, pistachios, coconut, pineapple, eggs, butter, vanilla, cinnamon and cardamom in bowl; mix well. Add bread cubes and toss gently. Let stand until bread soaks up cream mixture. Spoon mixture into prepared dish.

3. Bake 1 hour. Cool. Meanwhile, prepare Rum Raisin Sauce.

4. Cut warm or room temperature bread pudding into slices. Serve with Rum Raisin Sauce and sprinkle with powdered sugar, if desired.

Makes 12 servings

rum raisin sauce

1½ cups sugar
½ cup (1 stick) butter, melted
2 egg yolks, beaten
⅓ cup raisins
½ cup vanilla-flavored rum

Combine sugar and butter in medium saucepan and cook over low heat until sugar dissolves, stirring constantly. Remove from heat; stir about ¼ cup of mixture into egg yolks. Whisk egg yolks back into sugar mixture. Add raisins and rum; stir until well blended. Keep warm until ready to serve.

peanut butter squares

Sandra Portman, Buffalo Grove, IL

2½ cups powdered sugar
1¾ cups graham cracker crumbs
1 jar (8 ounces) creamy or chunky peanut butter
1 cup (2 sticks) butter or margarine, melted
1 teaspoon vanilla
1 package (12 ounces) milk chocolate chips

1. Combine powdered sugar, cracker crumbs, peanut butter, butter and vanilla in large bowl; mix well. Spread into 13×9-inch baking pan. Refrigerate until firm.

2. Place chocolate chips in microwavable dish. Microwave chips according to package directions. Spread over peanut butter mixture.

Makes 12 to 14 squares

gramma's cannoli cassata

Lois Gehrman, Crescent City, CA

6 cups whipping cream
2 eggs, slightly beaten
1 cup sugar
1 cup all-purpose flour
1 teaspoon grated lemon peel
½ cup finely chopped dried fruit
½ cup ricotta cheese
½ cup rum
¼ cup chopped pecans
2 teaspoons vanilla
1 pound cake (16 ounces), cut into ½-inch cubes

1. Whisk cream and eggs in medium saucepan just until blended. Add sugar, flour and lemon peel; stirring until well blended. Cook 5 to 10 minutes over medium heat, stirring constantly, or until mixture begins to thicken. Remove from heat; stir in dried fruit, ricotta cheese, rum, pecans and vanilla.

2. Place ⅓ of pound cake in tall trifle dish or deep serving bowl, distributing pieces to cover the bottom of the bowl. Top with ⅓ of cream mixture. Repeat layers 2 more times, ending with cream mixture. Cover with plastic wrap and refrigerate 4 hours or overnight. Serve cold.

Makes 12 servings

gramma's cannoli cassata

chocolate mousse

Helen Fan, Cupertino, CA

1 package (8 ounces) semisweet chocolate chips, melted
6 tablespoons unsalted butter, softened
¼ cup coffee
3 eggs, separated
½ cup whipping cream
¼ cup superfine sugar
  Whipped cream (optional)

1. Beat chocolate chips, butter and coffee in medium bowl with electric mixer at medium speed until blended. Beat in egg yolks, one at a time.

2. Beat whipping cream in small deep bowl with electric mixer at high speed until soft peaks form. Refrigerate until ready to use.

3. Beat egg whites in medium bowl at high speed until soft peaks form. Add sugar, 1 tablespoon at a time. Beat until stiff peaks form and mixture is shiny.

4. Fold egg whites into cream mixture. Fold chocolate mixture into cream mixture. Cover and chill 4 hours. Garnish with whipped cream, if desired.   *Makes 6 servings*

Helpful Hint: **Superfine sugar is finely granulated so it dissolves more readily. Use it for beverages, meringues and sweetened whipped cream.**

marty ann's famous southern pumpkin cheesecake

Marty Ann Roark, Las Vegas, NV

1¾ cups graham cracker crumbs
1 cup sugar, divided
½ cup (1 stick) butter or maragine, melted
1 package (8 ounces) cream cheese, softened
2 eggs, beaten
¾ cup milk
2 packages (3½ ounces each) French vanilla-flavored instant pudding mix
2 cups mashed fresh pumpkin or canned solid pack pumpkin
⅛ teaspoon ground cinnamon
1 container (12 ounces) frozen whipped topping, thawed and divided
Dash nutmeg

1. Preheat oven to 350°F.

2. Combine cracker crumbs, ¼ cup sugar and butter in small bowl. Press into bottom of 9-inch springform pan. Set aside.

3. Beat cream cheese, eggs and remaining ¾ cup sugar 2 minutes in medium bowl with electric mixer at medium speed until fluffy. Pour over crust. Bake 20 minutes; cool on wire rack.

4. Combine milk and pudding mix in large bowl. Beat 2 minutes with electric mixer at medium speed. Add pumpkin and cinnamon; mix well. Stir in 1 cup whipped topping.

5. Spread pudding mixture over cream cheese layer. Spread remaining whipped topping over pudding layer. Sprinkle with nutmeg. Refrigerate 4 hours or overnight.   *Makes 12 to 15 servings*

mom's apple crisp

Kim Carroll, Hastings, MN

4 cups peeled, thinly sliced Granny Smith apples
½ cup granulated sugar
½ cup plus 1 tablespoon all-purpose flour, divided
½ teaspoon ground cinnamon
½ cup uncooked quick oats
½ cup packed brown sugar
½ teaspoon baking soda
¼ teaspoon salt
⅛ teaspoon baking powder
¼ cup butter, softened
Vanilla ice cream (optional)

1. Preheat oven to 350°F. Spray 9×9-inch baking dish with nonstick cooking spray. Set aside.

2. Combine apples, sugar, 1 tablespoon flour and cinnamon in large bowl. Pour into prepared pan.

3. Combine remaining ½ cup flour, oats, brown sugar, baking soda, salt and baking powder in large bowl. Cut in butter with pastry blender or two knives until mixture resembles coarse crumbs. Sprinkle over apple mixture.

4. Bake 35 minutes or until hot and bubbly. Serve warm with ice cream, if desired.

Makes 4 servings

vanilla ice cream loaf

Helen Fan, Cupertino, CA

¼ cup powdered sugar
1 to 2 teaspoons water
1 package (3 ounces) ladyfingers
1½ quarts vanilla ice cream, softened
Raspberry or strawberry sauce, for garnish

1. Line 9×5-inch loaf pan with plastic wrap leaving 2½-inch overhang on all sides. Combine powdered sugar and water in small bowl; mix until mixture resembles paste.

2. Split ladyfingers. Spread small amount of powdered sugar mixture on bottom of 1 ladyfinger and anchor it upright against side of pan. Repeat with remaining ladyfingers, making border around pan.

3. Beat ice cream in large bowl with electric mixer until smooth. Spread into pan, pressing against ladyfingers. Cover and freeze 6 hours.

4. Place in refrigerator 20 minutes before serving. To serve place 1 tablespoon sauce on individual serving plates. Cut Ice Cream Loaf into 8 slices; place on sauce. Drizzle another 1 tablespoon sauce over top.   *Makes 8 servings*

raspberry bars

Elsie Brodjeski, Mentone, CA

1¼ cups all-purpose flour
¾ cup sugar, divided
½ cup (1 stick) butter or margarine, cut into ½-inch pieces
1 egg
2 egg whites
¾ cup chopped pecans
¾ cup raspberry jelly or jam

1. Preheat oven to 350°F. Grease 9-inch square baking pan; set aside.

2. Combine flour and ¼ cup sugar in medium bowl. Add butter; rub into flour mixture with fingers until fine crumbs form. Add egg; mix with fork until dough holds together. Pat into smooth ball. Firmly press dough evenly into bottom of prepared pan. Bake 20 to 25 minutes or until crust is pale golden in color.

3. Meanwhile, beat egg whites in medium bowl with electric mixer at high speed until soft peaks form. Beat in remaining ½ cup sugar until glossy; fold in pecans.

4. Spread jelly evenly over warm crust. Spread egg white mixture over jelly.

5. Bake 25 minutes more or until top is lightly browned. Cool completely on wire rack. Cut into bars.

Makes about 16 bars

raspberry bars

apricot fluff shortcakes

Mavis Gannello, Oak Park, IL

2 cups frozen whipped topping, thawed
4 tablespoons apricot preserves
5 shortcake shells (1 ounce each)
1 cup fresh blueberries
1 tablespoon sugar

1. Beat whipped topping and apricot preserves in large bowl with electric mixer at low speed until well blended. Place dollop on each shortcake shell.

2. Combine blueberries and sugar in small bowl. Place each shortcake on individual serving plates. Sprinkle blueberries over whipped topping and shortcakes.   *Makes 5 servings*

graham cracker pudding

Margaret L. Rose, Mentor on the Lake, OH

3 packages (4-serving size each) vanilla-flavored pudding mixes (not instant), plus milk to prepare
1 package (15 ounces) graham cracker crumbs
1½ cups light brown sugar, divided
3 large bananas, divided

1. Prepare pudding mixes according to package directions.

2. Sprinkle ⅓ of cracker crumbs on bottom of 13×9-inch baking pan. Sprinkle ½ cup brown sugar over crumbs. Slice 1 banana over brown sugar. Spread half of pudding over bananas. Repeat twice. Refrigerate until ready to serve.   *Makes 12 to 14 servings*

very berry trifle

Carole Resnick, Cleveland, OH

1 prepared sponge cake (10 inches)
5 cups whipping cream, divided
1 cup seedless red raspberry preserves
5 cups assorted fresh or thawed frozen berries
¼ cup granulated sugar
1 cup shredded coconut
3 tablespoons powdered sugar

1. Cut cake into ½-inch cubes. Place half of cake cubes on bottom of 3-quart trifle dish or bowl; set aside.

2. Beat 3 cups cream in medium bowl with electric mixer at high speed until stiff peaks form. Gently fold preserves into whipped cream; set aside.

3. Combine berries and granulated sugar in medium bowl. Let stand 10 minutes; drain accumulated liquid.

4. Spoon half of cream mixture over cake cubes. Carefully spoon half of berry mixture over cream mixture; sprinkle with ½ cup coconut. Repeat layers with remaining cake cubes, cream mixture, berry mixture and ½ cup coconut.

5. Beat remaining 2 cups cream and powdered sugar in medium bowl with electric mixer at high speed until stiff peaks form.

6. Reserve ¾ cup whipped cream mixture. Spread remaining 1¼ cups over trifle. Spoon reserved ¾ cup whipped cream into pastry bag fitted with large start tip. Pipe decorative dollops of whipped cream onto top of trifle. Refrigerate until ready to serve. *Makes 12 servings*

winter warm-up custard

Marla Hyatt, St. Paul, MN

3 cups whipping cream, divided
1 vanilla bean
7 egg yolks
½ cup plus 2 tablespoons sugar, divided
1 package (12 ounces) miniature semisweet chocolate chips, divided
6 ounces toffee-flavored baking chips, divided
¼ cup rum
1 teaspoon raspberry extract
2 cups boiling water
1 tablespoon sour cream
1 cup fresh raspberries

1. Preheat oven to 325°F.

2. Heat 2 cups whipping cream in medium saucepan over medium-high heat. Slice vanilla bean in half lengthwise and scrape seeds into cream; add vanilla bean pod to cream. Bring to a boil. Remove from heat; cool to 110°F.

3. Meanwhile, lightly beat egg yolks and ½ cup sugar in medium bowl with whisk. Whisk egg yolk mixture into cream mixture. Add 1 cup chocolate chips to saucepan; cook over low heat until chips melt, stirring occasionally, until mixture is smooth. Remove from heat. Stir in all but 2 tablespoons toffee chips, rum and raspberry extract, stirring until toffee chips melt. Divide evenly among six (4-ounce) custard cups.

4. Place custard cups in 13×9-inch baking dish; place in oven; carefully pour boiling water into pan around custard cups. Bake 45 minutes or until custard knife inserted into centers comes out clean. Top warm custard with remaining 1 cup chocolate chips and 2 tablespoons toffee chips. Cool completely or serve warm.

5. Beat remaining 1 cup whipping cream, 2 tablespoons sugar and sour cream until soft peaks form. Divide among custard cups; top with raspberries and serve immediately.

Makes 6 servings

lemony layers

Constance McMorris, Newberry, SC

> 3 eggs, separated
> 1 cup sugar
> ¼ cup all-purpose flour
> ½ cup milk
> 4 tablespoons lemon juice
> 2 tablespoons butter, melted
>   Whipped cream (optional)

1. Preheat oven to 350°F.

2. Beat egg yolks in large bowl with electric mixer at medium speed until light and fluffy. Add sugar, flour, milk and lemon juice. Beat until smooth. Stir in butter.

3. Beat egg whites in medium bowl until stiff peaks form. Fold into egg yolk mixture.

4. Pour into 1½-quart casserole dish. Bake 40 minutes or until top is lightly browned. Serve warm or cold. Top with whipped cream, if desired.

Makes 6 to 8 servings

frozen mocha dessert

Nancy Anderson, Yarmouth Port, MA

1 cup chocolate cookie crumbs (about 18 chocolate wafer cookies)
3 tablespoons margarine or butter, melted
¼ cup instant coffee granules
2 tablespoons hot water
3 packages (3 ounces each) reduced-fat cream cheese, softened
1 can (14 ounces) fat-free sweetened condensed milk
¾ cup reduced-calorie chocolate syrup
2 containers (8 ounces each) frozen whipped topping, thawed

1. Combine cookie crumbs and margarine in medium bowl. Press onto bottom of 10-inch springform pan. Chill.

2. Dissolve instant coffee in hot water in small bowl. Beat cream cheese 1 minute in medium bowl with electric mixer at medium speed until fluffy. Beat in coffee mixture, condensed milk and chocolate syrup until blended. Carefully fold in whipped topping until well blended.

3. Pour filling into prepared pan and tap gently on counter to remove air bubbles. Cover with plastic wrap; place in freezer at least 6 hours. Garnish and serve as desired.   *Makes 12 servings*

frozen mocha dessert

cranberry dessert

Karen Schmidt, Racine, WI

1½ cups sugar
½ cup (1 stick) butter, softened
2 eggs
1 cup all-purpose flour
1 teaspoon baking powder
2 cups fresh or frozen whole cranberries
¾ cup chopped nuts
   Vanilla ice cream or whipped topping (optional)

1. Preheat oven to 350°F. Grease 10-inch pie plate. Set aside.

2. Beat sugar, butter and eggs 2 minutes in medium bowl with electric mixer at medium speed. Stir in flour and baking powder. Stir in cranberries and nuts. (Dough will be stiff.) Spread into prepared pan.

3. Bake 45 minutes or until toothpock inserted in center comes out clean. Serve with ice cream or whipped cream, if desired.

Makes 10 to 12 servings

Helpful Hint: **Do not thaw the cranberries before using them in this recipe. Instead use them frozen.**

french vanilla bread pudding

Margaret D. Volk, LeRoy, IL

   2 cups french vanilla coffee cream
   1 cup sugar
   ½ cup (1 stick) butter
   5 eggs, slightly beaten, *or* 1¼ cups cholesterol-free egg substitute
   1 pound day-old unfrosted cinnamon rolls, cut into 1-inch cubes
   1 cup raisins
   ½ cup chopped pecans (optional)
   1 can (21 ounces) country apple or cherry pie filling
   Whipped Topping

1. Preheat oven to 350°F. Grease 13×9-inch pan. Set aside.

2. Combine coffee cream, sugar and butter in medium saucepan. Heat over medium heat until butter is melted, stirring occasionally. Cool; whisk in eggs.

3. Place bread cubes and raisins in prepared pan. Pour egg mixture over bread cubes. Allow egg mixture to soak into bread cubes, stirring occasionally. Sprinkle pecans, if desired, over bread mixture. Bake 30 minutes or until set. Cool. Top with pie filling and whipped topping.

Makes 12 servings

banana split cake

Tami Crosby, Glendale, AZ

1¼ cups sugar, divided
½ cup (1 stick) margarine, softened
1 package graham crackers (about 20)
2 packages (8 ounces each) cream cheese, softened
4 to 5 bananas
1 can (20 ounces) crushed pineapple, drained
1 container (12 ounces) frozen whipped topping, thawed
¼ cup chopped pecans or walnuts

1. Beat ¼ cup sugar and margarine in medium bowl with electric mixer at medium speed until creamed. Finely crush graham crackers in resealable plastic food storage bag with rolling pin. Add to margarine mixture. Press into bottom of well greased 13×9-inch baking dish.

2. Beat cream cheese and remaining 1 cup sugar 2 minutes in medium bowl with electric mixer at medium speed until creamy. Spread over cracker crust. Slice bananas and layer over cream cheese mixture. Spread pineapple over bananas. Spread whipped topping over pineapple. Sprinkle with pecans. Cover and chill 4 to 6 hours. *Makes 8 servings*

date loaf

Harriet E. Smith, Ocala, FL

1 package (8 ounces) pitted dates
2 cups miniature marshmallows
1 cup milk
2 cups graham cracker crumbs, divided
1 cup chopped pecans (optional)
   Whipped topping (optional)

1. Chop dates; set aside. Combine marshmallows and milk in medium bowl. Allow marshmallows to absorb some of the milk. Add dates, 1½ cups graham cracker crumbs and pecans, if desired; mix well. (Mixture will be moist.)

2. Sprinkle ¼ cup graham cracker crumbs on waxed paper. Place date mixture on waxed paper and shape into loaf. Sprinkle remaining ¼ cup graham cracker crumbs over top and sides of loaf. Wrap in foil and refrigerate until firm. Slice and serve with whipped topping, if desired.

Makes 8 to 10 servings

Helpful Hint: **Chopped pitted dates are a great timesaver in this date loaf. They are available in most large supermarkets. The easiest way to prepare whole dates for this recipe is to cut them into pieces with kitchen shears.**

cookie crumb sundae

Carrie Vredenburg, Olathe, KS

1 package (about 18 ounces) chocolate creme-filled sandwich cookies
4 cups milk, divided
1 package (4-serving size) chocolate fudge-flavored instant pudding mix
1 package (4-serving size) cheesecake-flavored instant pudding mix
1 container (8 ounces) frozen whipped topping, thawed
12 to 16 maraschino cherries, drained

1. Place cookies in large resealable plastic food storage bag and crush with rolling pin. Place ¾ of crumbs in bottom of 13×9-inch baking pan.

2. Combine 2 cups milk and cheesecake-flavored pudding mix in large bowl. Prepare according to package directions. Pour pudding evenly over cookie crumbs.

3. Repeat with remaining 2 cups milk and chocolate fudge-flavored pudding mix. Pour evenly over cheesecake pudding.

4. Spread whipped topping over pudding. Sprinkle remaining cookie crumbs over whipped topping. Top with maraschino cherries. Chill 1 hour before serving. *Makes 12 to 14 servings*

Carrie says: This dessert can also be made in individual disposable clear plastic cups. Decorate each with colored sprinkles. Kids love them like this. They are great for birthdays, holidays and picnics.

cookie crumb sundaes

noodle pudding

Laura Fitzgerald, New City, NY

> 4 cups ricotta cheese
> 2 cups sour cream
> 1½ cups sugar
> 8 eggs, beaten
> 1 can (20 ounces) crushed pineapple, drained
> 1 teaspoon vanilla
> 1 package (10 ounces) egg noodles, cooked and drained
> 4 cups milk, divided

1. Preheat oven to 350°F. Grease 13×9-inch baking dish. Set aside.

2. Combine cheese, sour cream, sugar, eggs, pineapple and vanilla in bowl; stir until blended. Fold in noodles. Pour into prepared pan. Bake, covered, 1 hour or until set.   *Makes 12 to 14 servings*

ambrosia

Laura Fitzgerald, New City, NY

> 1 package (4-serving size) gelatin, any flavor
> 1 cup boiling water
> 1 can (20 ounces) crushed pineapple, drained and juice reserved
> 1 can (11 ounces) mandarin oranges, drained and juice reserved
> 1 container (16 ounces) sour cream
> ½ cup shredded coconut
> 1 cup miniature marshmallows

Prepare gelatin according to package directions using boiling water and substituting reserved juices for cold water. Add sour cream to gelatin; whisk until smooth. Stir in fruit and coconut. Top with marshmallows. Refrigerate until firm.   *Makes 8 to 10 servings*

blueberry shortcakes with apricot crème

Mavis Gannello, Oak Park, IL

   1 container (8 ounces) frozen whipped topping, thawed and divided
   4 tablespoons apricot preserves
   5 (1-ounce) shortcake shells
   1 cup fresh blueberries
   1 tablespoon sugar

1. Reserve ½ cup whipped topping. Beat remaining whipped topping and apricot preserves in large bowl with electric mixer on low speed until light and fluffy. Divide evenly among shortcakes.

2. Reserve 5 large blueberries for garnish. Place remaining blueberries in small bowl. Sprinkle with sugar; toss gently. Divide among shortcakes. Top each cake with about 1 tablespoon reserved whipped topping and 1 reserved blueberry.   *Makes 5 servings*

strawberry angel food dessert

Mardel Barnette, Comstock, WI

   3 packages (4-serving size) strawberry-flavored gelatin mix
   4 cups boiling water
   2 packages (16 ounces each) frozen strawberries
   1 angel food cake
   1 container (4 ounces) frozen whipped topping, thawed

1. Combine gelatin mix and water in large bowl. Stir until gelatin is dissolved. Add strawberries; stir until strawberries are thawed. Let stand until thickened.

2. Tear angel food cake into small pieces. Fold into strawberry mixture. Fold in whipped topping. Spread cake mixture into 15×11-inch pan. Chill.   *Makes 12 to 15 servings*

daddy's favorite pineapple pudding

Mary G. Taylor, Murfreesboro, TN

1¾ cups sugar, divided
½ cup all-purpose flour
2½ cups milk
¼ cup margarine
3 eggs, separated
1 teaspoon vanilla
1 can (20 ounces) pineapple chunks, drained and juice reserved
½ bag vanilla wafers

1. Preheat oven to 375°F. Combine 1½ cups sugar and flour in medium saucepan. Add milk, margarine, egg yolks and vanilla. Bring to a boil, stirring constantly. Add reserved pineapple juice. Bring to a boil. Remove from heat; stir in pineapple chunks.

2. Line 13×9-inch baking dish with vanilla wafers. Pour pineapple mixture over wafers. Beat egg whites in medium bowl until soft peaks form. Add remaining ¼ cup sugar and beat until stiff peaks form. Spread over pudding. Bake 8 to 10 minutes or until top is lightly browned.

Makes 12 servings

dixie dream

Lois Dowling, Tacoma, WA

- **1 cup semisweet chocolate chips, melted**
- **1 cup dry roasted peanuts, finely chopped**
- **1 cup peanut butter, divided**
- **1 cup white chocolate chips, melted**
- **1 cup cream cheese, softened**
- **3 cups whipped topping, divided**

1. Grease 11-inch round plate or pizza pan. Combine chocolate chips, peanuts and ¾ cup peanut butter in medium bowl. Press onto prepared plate; chill until firm.

2. Beat remaining ¼ cup peanut butter, white chocolate chips and cream cheese in medium bowl until fluffy. Fold in 2 cups whipped topping. Spread over crust. Decorate with remaining 1 cup whipped topping. Refrigerate until ready to serve.   *Makes 12 servings*

nicy icy dessert

Elinor Jane Smith, Ocala, FL

- **½ gallon vanilla frozen yogurt, softened**
- **¼ cup sugar-free maple syrup**
- **1 can (11 ounces) mandarin oranges, drained**
- **½ cup seedless grapes**
- **½ cup toasted pecans, broken into pieces**
- **Maraschino cherries (optional)**

Place yogurt into large serving bowl. Swirl in maple syrup. Fold in oranges, grapes and pecans. Freeze until firm. Serve with maraschino cherries, if desired.   *Makes 10 servings*

INDEX

METRIC CONVERSION CHART

VOLUME MEASUREMENTS (dry)

$1/8$ teaspoon = 0.5 mL
$1/4$ teaspoon = 1 mL
$1/2$ teaspoon = 2 mL
$3/4$ teaspoon = 4 mL
1 teaspoon = 5 mL
1 tablespoon = 15 mL
2 tablespoons = 30 mL
$1/4$ cup = 60 mL
$1/3$ cup = 75 mL
$1/2$ cup = 125 mL
$2/3$ cup = 150 mL
$3/4$ cup = 175 mL
1 cup = 250 mL
2 cups = 1 pint = 500 mL
3 cups = 750 mL
4 cups = 1 quart = 1 L

VOLUME MEASUREMENTS (fluid)

1 fluid ounce (2 tablespoons) = 30 mL
4 fluid ounces ($1/2$ cup) = 125 mL
8 fluid ounces (1 cup) = 250 mL
12 fluid ounces ($1 1/2$ cups) = 375 mL
16 fluid ounces (2 cups) = 500 mL

WEIGHTS (mass)

$1/2$ ounce = 15 g
1 ounce = 30 g
3 ounces = 90 g
4 ounces = 120 g
8 ounces = 225 g
10 ounces = 285 g
12 ounces = 360 g
16 ounces = 1 pound = 450 g

DIMENSIONS

$1/16$ inch = 2 mm
$1/8$ inch = 3 mm
$1/4$ inch = 6 mm
$1/2$ inch = 1.5 cm
$3/4$ inch = 2 cm
1 inch = 2.5 cm

OVEN TEMPERATURES

250°F = 120°C
275°F = 140°C
300°F = 150°C
325°F = 160°C
350°F = 180°C
375°F = 190°C
400°F = 200°C
425°F = 220°C
450°F = 230°C

BAKING PAN SIZES

Utensil	Size in Inches/Quarts	Metric Volume	Size in Centimeters
Baking or	$8 \times 8 \times 2$	2 L	$20 \times 20 \times 5$
Cake Pan	$9 \times 9 \times 2$	2.5 L	$23 \times 23 \times 5$
(square or	$12 \times 8 \times 2$	3 L	$30 \times 20 \times 5$
rectangular)	$13 \times 9 \times 2$	3.5 L	$33 \times 23 \times 5$
Loaf Pan	$8 \times 4 \times 3$	1.5 L	$20 \times 10 \times 7$
	$9 \times 5 \times 3$	2 L	$23 \times 13 \times 7$
Round Layer	$8 \times 1 1/2$	1.2 L	20×4
Cake Pan	$9 \times 1 1/2$	1.5 L	23×4
Pie Plate	$8 \times 1 1/4$	750 mL	20×3
	$9 \times 1 1/4$	1 L	23×3
Baking Dish	1 quart	1 L	—
or Casserole	$1 1/2$ quart	1.5 L	—
	2 quart	2 L	—